COOKING **WITH** AND **WITHOUT** A RECIPE

CHEF AT HOME

COOKING **WITH** AND **WITHOUT** A RECIPE

CHEF AT HOME

MICHAEL SMITH

whitecap

Whitecap Books is known for its expertise in the cookbook market, and has produced some of the most innovative and familiar titles found in kitchens across North America. Visit our website at www.whitecap.ca.

Edited by Elaine Jones
Proofread by Joan E. Templeton
Design by Stacey Noyes / LuzForm Design
Photographs by Alanna Jankov and Loretta Campbell
Food Styling by Rachel Leslie and Tommy Archibald

Printed and bound in Hong Kong

LIBRARY AND ARCHIVES CANADA CATALOGUING IN PUBLICATION

Smith, Michael, 1966–
      Chef at home / Michael Smith.

Includes index.
ISBN 1-55285-716-6
ISBN 978-1-55285-716-8

      1. Cookery. I. Title.

TX714.S595 2005   641.5   C2005-903041-0

The publisher acknowledges the financial support of the Government of Canada through the Book Publishing Industry Development Program (BPIDP) and the Province of British Columbia through the Book Publishing Tax Credit.

This book is for Rachel and Gabe.
Thanks for teaching me how to really cook!
It's also for your family.
I know they'll love it too!

CONTENTS

REAL COOKING 101
FAMILY, FRIENDS AND FOOD

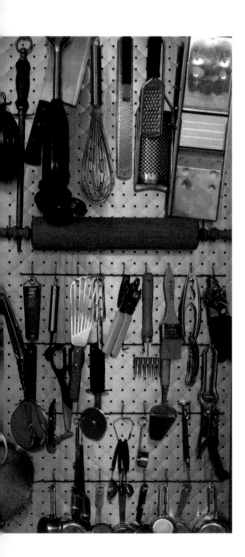

I LOVE FOOD. I LOVE COOKING IT. I LOVE EATING IT. For me it's always a celebration. In the kitchens of my life great ingredients, prepared simply and shared with family and friends, have always inspired me to be my best.

Since I can't come to your house to cook—and even if I did I'd want to eat your food, not mine—I share my passion through my cooking show "Chef at Home" and this book. They both reflect my journey from home cook to professional cook—and back to home cook. It's been quite a ride!

My mom kick-started my cookie-baking career early by letting me help her instead of shooing me off like the three-year-old mess-maker I was. Since then I've learned a thing or two. I've discovered that nothing jazzes me up more than cooking for my partner, Rachel, and my son, Gabe. I've learned that my son's dinner is way more important than a hundred-dollar tasting menu. I've found that I love the quiet satisfaction of cooking tasty, healthy meals for my family. I don't miss the long hours of a restaurant kitchen but I sure do miss professional dishwashers!

I've been a professional chef for the past 20 years and I've seen a few things along the way. I've had the privilege of cooking on three continents, in the city and the country, on planes, trains and ships. I've had the honour of cooking for kings, queens and presidents. I even ran away with the circus once to cook for them. I've seen enough melted chocolate to fill a swimming pool, peeled a mountain of onions, and washed more dishes than an army cook. But it's all just been a warm-up for my favourite job: home cook.

As a father I really appreciate the tremendous challenges we all face taking care of our families. But I also know that most of what makes me a good home cook has nothing to do with being a pro.

I didn't know it at the time but the many cookie batters I ruined as a kid taught me my first important lesson—have fun in the kitchen. It's a friendly place. No stress, no rules. Doesn't every kid want to play with food? Experiment? I was lucky. My mom encouraged it! That feeling is now hard-wired in my cooking style. It can be a part of your style too. I know cooking can seem a bit intimidating at times. What else do you do every day that's so full of puzzle pieces? Unpronounceable ingredients, scientific techniques, specific tools and a table full of critics can scare the apron off any cook. But you don't need vast resources at your disposal to be a good home cook.

You don't have to wear a chef's jacket to take care of your family! Quite the contrary. All you need is a table full of family and friends and a free kitchen spirit.

My kitchen is full of quiet confidence, healthy choices and raucous flavour. And yours can be too. It's simple. Let your instincts be your guide. Improvise your family's meals from what's already in your refrigerator and pantry. Be a chef at home—you can do it!

MY SECRET RECIPE?
COOKING WITH AND WITHOUT A RECIPE!

YOU DON'T NEED A RECIPE to cook a wonderful meal. Just let your appetite and your instincts be your guide.

In recent years we've lost much of our hands-on cooking tradition. Many of us don't cook as much as our parents did, and when we do find the time we're often stressed out. What's this ingredient? How do I cook it? Does it taste good? Is it good for me? Will my kids eat it? Many cooks need a reference, a gold standard to turn to for guaranteed results. Enter the recipe as we know it today.

Recipes are how cooks share ideas. In this cookbook they're also the starting point for your own food journey. Your meal is the destination, not mine, so don't feel like you have to follow my recipes perfectly to reach success. They're just a road map. Let them pave the way for you to teach yourself. Enjoy the scenery as your own kitchen confidence builds. You'll have lots of fun and enjoy some pretty tasty results along the way.

You can use this book in many different ways. It's loaded with ideas that your family will enjoy the first time you make them. You'll discover that the recipes are also a way to try out a new style of cooking. A style that values your input—not just mine. Turn this book into a scrapbook for your own inevitable ideas. Like my television series, this book was created to help you be creative. Roll up your sleeves and dive in. You just might impress yourself in your own kitchen!

This book is meant to be ripped, oil-stained, accidentally burnt and deliberately written on. It works best in the kitchen—not on your coffee table. If you shake it and a cloud of whole grain flour or a few fennel seeds fall out, then it's working!

HOW TO COOK
WITHOUT A RECIPE

THE RECIPES IN THIS BOOK are just words on paper. They include more than enough detail to get you started but not too much to stop the personality of your kitchen from shining through. They're full of all the information you need to guarantee a tasty meal, but they also leave lots of room for experimentation. Have fun making them your own! Here are a few tips . . .

START WITH GREAT INGREDIENTS

It's the key to all great cooking. Great ingredients will let your food shine. No amount of fancy technique and expensive cookware can make up for a piece of tough beef. Choose fresh, local and organic ingredients if you can find them. Would you prefer organic free-range beef or the trim from a tough old dairy cow?

MEASURE LOOSELY

None of these recipes rely on rigid precision for success. When measurements are too specific they seem to suggest that there's only one way to cook—the writer's way. Not true! Your idea of a pinch, a spoonful or a cup may be different from mine, but that's our goal. Any two cooks will get different results from the same recipe, but only yours will be personalized with your own kitchen spirit. Who cares if your stew is missing celery and has more carrots than mine? They'll both taste great!

BE BOLD

Most seasoning mistakes are made by adding too little of a particular flavour instead of too much. It's human nature to take baby steps into the unknown. I understand. But don't be tentative. Cooking is a lot more fun—and flavourful—when you throw caution to the wind. I don't like beef stew with a subtle red wine flavour. I like it with a lot!

SET A GOAL

What do you feel like eating? Look in your refrigerator or pantry. Leaf through this book until you find something you like. Go for it! Read the recipe introduction to get a sense of what makes it unique. Imagine how you want it to look and taste. Think about the big picture before sweating the details. In the mood for a hearty bowl of beef stew? Get ready to braise!

CHOOSE FLAVOURS THAT MATCH

Ask yourself: What would I like to eat? Then ask: What would I like with it? It's that simple. There are no magic rules. If you like the way flavours taste together, they work. Remember them, write them down in this book, and choose them again. For inspiration, look for ingredients that grow in the same part of the world, ingredients that are in season together, ingredients that traditionally go together, and even those that don't. Apples and acorn squash, chocolate and coffee, beef and Asian five-spice powder.

COOK WITH INSIGHT

Think about the steps ahead. Read the recipe and absorb the hints on why a particular method or technique works best for the ingredients. Understand that every ingredient is full of flavours waiting to be coaxed forward by great cooking. It'll help you understand why one ingredient goes with another, when something's done cooking, or why a certain ingredient is always handled the same way. You'll be as obsessed with browning meat for stew as I am!

KEEP IT SIMPLE

Don't confuse enthusiasm with complexity. Simple tastes best. Experiment and add flavours but don't go overboard. Sometimes leaving something out of the pot makes a dish taste better than adding it. Beef stew with three peppercorns, tarragon, rosemary, thyme, bay leaf, juniper, Cabernet and Pinot Noir might be a bit much!

EXPERIMENT

Every recipe in this book is ripe for experimentation. There may be a few steps that need to be done a specific way, but you'll also find many steps that can be modified as you please. Play with your ingredients–substitute one for another–you'll find all kinds of fun variations that'll belong to you. You'll realize that words on paper are no substitute for flavours on the plate. Beef stew scented with tarragon or rosemary? Water or stock? You choose, then go for it!

CHANGE A DISH— EVERY TIME YOU MAKE IT

Who says a great dish has to taste the same way every time you make it? Not me! That's boring. You can certainly repeat a flavour combination you enjoy, but a recipe doesn't need to be rigid to be perfect. I constantly tinker with amounts and look for ways to vary a dish I've become comfortable with. I wonder how beef stew would taste with a bit of horseradish in the mix? Maybe a different wine next time?

LISTEN!

Like any art or craft your cooking will get better with feedback. It's part of the creative process to listen to your family and friends. Their thoughts will help you improve. But if they don't like something, don't take it personally. Instead think about how you'll cook it the next time. Maybe beef stew with avocado mashed potatoes isn't such a good idea anyway!

14

KNOW YOUR INGREDIENTS

If a recipe isn't specific about what type of ingredient to use, feel free to use any kind. An onion is an onion no matter what colour or size it is.

Whatever you happen to have on hand will taste great. In general, I prefer the bright flavours of fresh herbs to the often dull flavours of dried ones. I use corn or canola oil for all-purpose cooking unless I specify flavourful olive oil. I

tend to use organic products whenever possible; they might cost a bit more but their tasty goodness is often worth it. If I ask you to use your favourite ingredient, pick the tastiest one you can find. I might use a Riesling wine instead of the Chardonnay you prefer, but they both taste great!

FEEL THE TEMPERATURE

You'll notice that I suggest a medium-high heat in many of the recipes. I usually don't cook with the highest heat setting on my stove because it burns things! High heat is really only good for boiling water. There's a magical sweet spot on every dial that's perfect for caramelizing and browning the simple sugars in almost all of the food you cook. Find it and you'll never burn a chicken breast or a pancake again!

SEASON LIKE A PRO

Salt and pepper are your best friends in the kitchen. They make the ordinary extraordinary. I prefer the crisp, clean taste of sea salt or Kosher salt to the chemical aftertaste of iodized salt. I find freshly ground pepper is best for adding spicy heat and aromatic flavour. I lightly season ingredients as they cook and then taste them when they're done and season again before serving.

HOW TO COOK **WITH** A RECIPE

THE RECIPES IN THIS BOOK are full of ideas and tips for using the resources in your own kitchen. The details you'll need are there. As you cook with them, feel free to interpret the instructions any way you'd like. The results will taste great wherever you go, and you'll be able to call them your own. Here are a few things to keep in mind.

MEASURE BY PINCHES, SPOONFULS AND CUPFULS

The recipes in this book usually don't ask you to use precise teaspoons, table-spoons or cupfuls. When they do it's because a precise measure will help the dish, like the amount of baking powder in a pancake for instance. Instead they suggest a general pinch, spoonful, cupful or even handful. Use your own judg-ment. Use a small spoon for less flavour or a big heaping one like I do for more flavour. But don't worry, the dish will taste great however you measure.

TASTE!

The best lesson I've learned in all my years of cooking is to taste food as I cook it—not just when it's done. At first you'll take note of general flavours, but with practice you'll gain important insight into what happens to ingredients as you cook them. Taste everything!

USE YOUR **FOOD** SENSE

SOMETIMES IN THE STORM of often-contradictory nutritional advice that comes our way we forget how easy it is to take care of our families. We get confused. Good potato? Bad potato? Help!

As a chef at home you can relax and cook your best. Cooking is an easy antidote to a processed-food lifestyle. You'll realize how easy it is to cook healthy, flavourful food for your family. You'll eat well and feel great!

Here are some guidelines. They're not rules. They just remind you of a few simple things that life has already taught you.

COOK FOR YOUR FAMILY

Sharing a meal with your family is one of the most powerful things you can do for each other. A strong family starts with individuals but grows together with time. Sit down and eat. Laugh, cry and share. Let your love for each other guide you to be your best in the kitchen.

SHOP SMART

You are what you eat. Easy. Fuel your machine with goodness. Since almost all the food decisions you make for your family are at the supermarket, be careful. Stay out of those aisles—you know the ones. Load your cart with healthy choices. Remember variety is not just the spice of life, it's the key to life! If you routinely bring home a wide range of fruits, vegetables, whole grains, fish, yogurt and other healthy goodies, someday you'll get the chance to teach your great-grandkids how to clean their plates!

GO FOR COLOUR!

We all know that fruits and vegetables are good for us, but did you know that the more colourful they are the better they are? That's right. Mother Nature packs vital nutrients into the pigments that give produce its signature palette. It's no coincidence that those bright colours catch our eye. Don't fight it! Give in to your colourful urges. Stick to your favourite fruits and vegetables, but try new ones too. An ever-growing variety in your life will energize your family for the long run.

SKIP DIETS

There's no such thing as a diet; it's a silly four-letter word. There's only lifestyle. You gain weight by eating more calories than you can burn. That's why it's so important to live an active life. We're hard-wired to go to great lengths to find food, eat every bit we can get our hands on, then store the rest for the future. Today, diet-peddlers suggest that a narrowly defined regimen of processed food and bland flavour will sustain us. Not true! There's no magic solution, but to avoid the pitfalls of the modern, sedentary lifestyle, exercise your food sense. Put as much effort into your daily activity as you do cooking and eating.

UNDERSTAND SLOW CARB POWER

Carbohydrates are the fuel for the engine; they're nature's energy source and vital for life. Unfortunately, we're surrounded by bad carbs that often overshadow good carbs. Slow carbs are the key. We're at our best when food gives us sustained energy. The best way to get essential long-burning carb energy is to eat whole grains every single day. As a bonus you'll also get lots of antioxidants, fibre, B-complex vitamins, minerals, protein and no saturated fat. You'll also help reduce your risk of heart disease, type-2 diabetes, and a laundry list of other preventable ailments. Whole grain power!

18

BUILD STRENGTH WITH PROTEIN

Protein is the fundamental building block of life. Plants make their own but animals can't. So we eat plants—or other animals. Hence our craving for steak and mushrooms. But the heavy, artery-clogging fats in red meat make it a once-a-week treat, not a daily staple. Fortunately, there are still thousands of other ways to find protein in nature, like lean meats, poultry, cheese, yogurt or the fish my family eats every week. Fish is loaded with the goodness of the ocean. It's fat-free, packed with healthy oils and tastes awesome. It's an excellent protein choice and so are some vegetables. Combine a whole grain with a bean at any meal and you'll be a protein-making machine!

TAKE A MULTIVITAMIN

There's no magic bullet for guaranteed health. Feed your body the way it's meant to be—with lots of whole grains, smart proteins, fruits and vegetables—and you'll get all the vitamins and minerals you need to flourish. But even the best cooks sometimes have inadvertent nutritional holes to plug. That's why most nutritionists recommend a multi-vitamin. Just in case. But never as a substitute.

MOTHER NATURE KNOWS BEST

Mother Nature has taken care of us for a long time, and we're at our best when our food is as close to her as possible. But sometimes we stray a bit. Great big factories full of artificial flavours, artificial fat and mounds of sugar and salt do us more harm than good. Stick to the basics–pure ingredients. If you can, buy wholesome, nutritious organic ingredients. They respect the environment and your health!

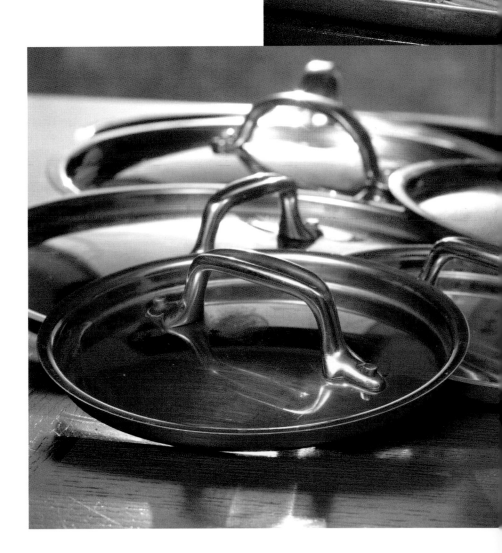

WATCH FOR PORTION DISTORTION

We're conditioned to eat as much as we can. A super-sized world can drown you in a sea of calories! Slow down and savour your food, let your body catch up to your appetite. Who says you have to clean your plate?

DRINK LOTS OF WATER

If food is the fuel for the engine, then water is the oil. It's part of virtually every metabolic process in our bodies and vital for health. Stay hydrated and everything just works better. Six to eight glasses a day will keep your machine running in peak condition!

REV UP YOUR FRIDGE,
PANTRY AND TOOL DRAWER

MY KITCHEN IS A BIT LIKE a mad scientist's lab. It often looks like a yard sale. Sometimes it smells funny. There are clear glass jars everywhere filled with a collection of odd potions, remnants from last year's herb garden and colourful powders from the far corners of the world. The drawers are bursting with forgotten tools and a growing chopstick collection. The refrigerator is a world unto itself; I can get lost in it for days!

Most kitchens are people and mess magnets. In mine, I can't turn around without bumping into a herd of kids, a pile of dirty dishes or a dusty pail of potatoes. The neighbourhood dogs stop by regularly. It's hosted a live lobster race and quite a few parties. Curious travellers and hungry neighbours come and go. Fortunately, memories stay. I love it. It's a fun place to cook.

My kitchen strategy is simple: lots of choices. I'm a flavour fanatic so I love being surrounded by tons of ingredients that I can use to spontaneously create a meal. You can too! Fill your shelves with a variety of flavours and you'll always be ready to be a chef at home. I love opening my refrigerator without knowing what I'm going to cook. It's always full of ideas and great ingredients—like my favourite aromatic fresh herbs, basil, cilantro, dill and parsley. If I spot a vegetable at the market that I haven't tasted in a while I bring it home. I even rescue stranded exotic stuff that can't find a home. I stock kitchen staples from other parts of the world so that anytime I feel like a little culinary tourism I can head for the Mediterranean or Southeast Asia. My refrigerator is like a culinary scrapbook full of leftover bits and a collection of condiments, vinaigrettes and sauces packed into jars.

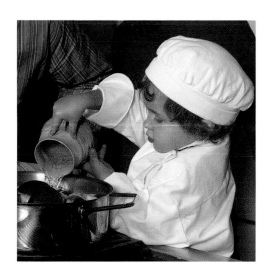

My freezer is always full of colourful berries and other smoothie fruit. I love grating frozen ginger into an aromatic powder, so there's usually a root or two buried in it somewhere. I always keep frozen butter on hand since I'm often overwhelmed by the urge to make biscuits, and nothing makes a flakier biscuit than frozen butter.

My pantry is my playground. I never know what's going to happen when I check the shelves. I love knowing that it's packed with bright flavours and ready to kick-start dinner. My ever-growing collection of herbs and spices sits quietly, each knowing its time will come. I keep enough whole grains to open a bakery, and my olive oil selection is the envy of any nutritionist.

My tool collection is my pride and joy. I've got everything I need to slice, dice, chop, mince, purée, cut, sift and strain anything from a simple onion to a rare Mexican jumping bean. I rely on a few simple pots, a sharp knife or two and my wooden cutting board, but I also keep a few fancy tools around. My microplane grater coaxes aromatic flavour from a parade of citrus skins, turns the hardest cheese (and frozen ginger) into a powder and usually leaves my knuckles intact. My fancy French mandoline shaves fennel into paper-thin slices and makes short work of potato slicing. My immersion blender can handle almost any puréeing job and is super-easy to clean up. If I ever need four whips at once or nine wooden spoons, I'm ready!

Of course, you're cooking dinner in your kitchen—not mine! But I'll bet it smells just as good and comes complete with any of the tools that you'll really need. And a little salt and pepper.

S N A C K S

WHEN YOUR APPETITE CALLS for a fast break, nothing beats the spontaneity of a high-speed snack. I love creating simple ones to keep me going, and I try out new flavours every chance I get. They're so easy to make it hardly feels like cooking.

Snacks are perfect for experimenting. Add your own flavours. Flex your creative muscles as a warm-up for the bigger meals! Snacks are good for you. They give you energy and are a great way to eat all kinds of nutritious food. And since they're easy to clean up, they pass the dirty-dish test with flying colours.

WHEN I WAS A LITTLE BOY a tuna sandwich was the very first thing in the kitchen I was allowed to make all by myself. I was very proud that I didn't need a helping hand—or a recipe! I know that you don't either, so think of this as a guide to jazzing up this kitchen classic with a few new flavours. The tried and true is a great place to start experimenting.

TUNA FISH SANDWICH

Flake the tuna with a fork, then mix it with the lemon juice, oil, mustard, onion, pickle, celery and parsley. Have a taste, then season to your liking with salt and pepper.

Spread a thick layer of the tuna salad on two slices of bread. Top with a layer of lettuce and crisp potato chips. Slap on the remaining bread. Press down a bit to even out the chips, then have a huge bite. Remember to share the other one!

FEEL FREE TO TRY

A sandwich should be quick and easy to make with whatever's in your kitchen. If you don't have lemon, a splash of any vinegar will add a bit of sharp flavour contrast. Any type of mustard or onion works well. I like to try fresh herbs other than parsley; tarragon and dill are two of my favourites. I sometimes top a sandwich with lettuce, cucumber or even vegetable sprouts. Of course, any bread will work too; try toasting your choice for a bit more crunch. Whatever you do though, make sure you try the chips!

HINTS

I prefer the rich fruity flavours of extra virgin olive oil to the blandness of mayonnaise. All canned tuna fish is good for you but I prefer water-packed to oil-packed and light tuna because it contains less mercury than albacore or white. Chunky or solid are both fine, since you'll shred them anyway.

A can of your favourite water-packed tuna, drained

A squeeze or two of lemon juice (and perhaps some of the zest)

A generous splash of olive oil

A spoonful of Dijon mustard

A spoonful of minced red onion

A spoonful of minced pickle

A spoonful of minced celery

A spoonful of chopped parsley

A sprinkle or two of salt and pepper

4 slices of whole wheat bread

A few lettuce leaves

A handful of potato chips

MAKES TWO SANDWICHES

THIS LEMONADE IS just as popular with grown-ups as it is with kids. Its pink colour comes from an old bartender's trick, bright red grenadine syrup. The balance of sweet and sour flavours is just the thing on a hot summer's day and it's not too sweet for seconds—or thirds!

PINK LEMONADE

For maximum fragrance and strong lemon flavour, zest the lemons into a small bowl, then add the juice. Whisk in the sugar and salt. It won't dissolve completely in the juice but will in the water.

Fill a two-quart pitcher halfway with ice cubes. Add the lemon syrup and top up with cold water. Stir in grenadine syrup until you like the colour.

Serve immediately and get ready to pass on the recipe!

8 lemons

A cupful of sugar

A pinch of salt

A splash or two of grenadine syrup

MAKES ABOUT EIGHT GLASSES

FEEL FREE TO TRY

If you prefer your lemonade a bit more tart, use a little less sugar. For a sparkling treat, replace the water with club soda. Grown-ups might enjoy a splash of gin or vodka in their glass!

HINTS

The skin of a lemon is loaded with aromatic lemon oil that adds a lot more flavour than the sour juice. Stay away from store-bought lemon juice if you can; its flavours are dull compared to the real thing. And not all lemons are juicy. To help juice hard ones after you're done zesting, try rolling them until you feel them loosen up. You can also microwave them for 20 seconds.

THE FIRST TIME I TOSSED a perfectly good watermelon with olive oil my partner, Rachel, thought I was nuts—until she tried it. The combination may sound a bit odd, but once you taste it you'll be hooked too. The sweetness of the melon is accented nicely by the salt, the heat of the pepper and the fruitiness of the olive oil.

28

SALT AND PEPPER WATERMELON

Half a watermelon, cut into large cubes

A generous splash or two of your best olive oil

A generous sprinkle of salt and pepper

SERVES FOUR

Toss the watermelon with the olive oil and lots of salt and pepper. I dare you to eat just one chunk!

FEEL FREE TO TRY

A small splash of balsamic vinegar or lime juice will add a balancing touch of sourness. Coarse salt—in particular coarse sea salt—adds a tantalizing crunchy texture.

HINTS

Use your very best extra virgin olive oil —its fruity, peppery flavours will sharpen the sweet watermelon.

THE BEST WAY TO EAT a garden-ripe tomato is by hand, like an apple, with no elaborate flavours to get in the way. But this is another great way to enjoy tomatoes—on a plate with a few simple flavourings. It's about as close to perfection as you can get in a kitchen.

A PLATEFUL OF TOMATOES

Slice the tomatoes thinly or thickly, whichever you prefer. Spread them out on a plate, then generously drizzle them with olive oil and lemon juice. Season liberally with lots of salt and pepper. Grab a fork and somebody to share with. Simple!

2 or 3 large ripe tomatoes

A splash or two of your best olive oil

A squeeze or two of fresh lemon juice

A sprinkle or two of salt and pepper

SERVES TWO

FEEL FREE TO TRY

For even more fresh garden flavour, try tossing a handful of whole fresh basil or mint leaves into the mix or replace the lemon with your favourite vinegar. Balsamic is my favourite. For a salad effect, add sliced avocados and either thinly sliced red onions or the Pickled Red Onions on page 165.

HINTS

Never refrigerate tomatoes! The cold prevents them from fully ripening and knocks out whatever fresh flavour they have. I keep mine on the windowsill and let the sun perk them up.

IN ITALY, BRUSCHETTA IS OFTEN just bread with garlic. In North America, we usually add a simple tomato topping. Either way the secret is great ingredients treated simply. Thick slices of rustic bread, toasted with aromatic olive oil, rubbed with pungent garlic, then topped with ripe tomatoes and herbs. Awesome!

BRUSCHETTA

Cut the bread into thick slices. Drizzle each one with lots of olive oil. If you have a grill, fire it up and toast the slices until they're light golden brown. If you don't have a grill, lay them on a baking pan and toast them in a 375°F (190°C) oven until golden brown, about 10 to 15 minutes. Before each slice cools too much, vigorously rub it with the cut surface of a garlic clove.

Meanwhile, roughly chop the herb leaves and toss them with the tomatoes and onion. Add a generous splash of olive oil and season with salt and pepper. Spoon some topping onto each slice and pass around. Enjoy!

FEEL FREE TO TRY

Add some chopped kalamata-style olives or grated Parmesan to the tomato topping. A quick squeeze of lemon juice will balance tomatoes that are very sweet. A handful of fresh tarragon leaves adds a delightful licorice-like flavour. If your tomatoes need a boost, add a spoonful of tomato paste.

HINTS

Rubbing raw garlic on the bread adds aroma but not overwhelming pungency. Keep an eye on it as it bakes: if a few slices toast faster then the others pull them out first and leave the rest for a few minutes longer.

A loaf of Itallan or French bread

A few splashes of your best olive oil

A clove or two of garlic, cut in half lengthwise

A handful or two of fresh basil, oregano or flat-leaf parsley

A few diced ripe tomatoes

A sliced red onion or a few sliced green onions

Another splash of your best olive oil

A sprinkle or two of salt and pepper

MAKES ENOUGH FOR FOUR

A FRESHLY TOSSED SALSA of juicy ripe tomatoes and aromatic flavours is an easy-to-make, easy-to-enjoy snack. Sweet tomatoes, pungent onions, sour lime, aromatic herbs, salt and spicy pepper all balance each other in a vibrant harmony of tastes. A good salsa doesn't ruin your day with too much spicy heat; it brightens it with just enough! Serve it with your favourite dipping chips.

FRESH SALSA

2 or 3 chopped ripe tomatoes

1 minced chili pepper

The juice and zest of 1 or 2 limes

A handful of cilantro leaves

A big splash of your best olive oil

A few thinly sliced green onions

A heaping spoonful of tomato paste

A spoonful of ground cumin seed

A sprinkle or two of salt

MAKES A FEW CUPS

Toss everything together until well combined. Try not to eat it all in one sitting!

To save time, and for a texture twist, simply pulse everything together in your food processor.

FEEL FREE TO TRY

There are many types of chili peppers, each with its own heat level and flavour. I prefer medium-heat varieties like poblano and jalapeño. You may want to substitute freshly grated ginger for the chili peppers. Cilantro is the classic fresh herb in salsa, but basil, oregano and even parsley work well too. The sweet pungency of a red onion is a great replacement for green onions.

HINTS

Garden tomatoes have the most flavour—when they're in season. If they're not in season, look for organic or vine-attached types, then take them home and ripen them for a few days on a sunny windowsill. In a pinch, a small can of whole tomatoes is more flavourful than a few hard, unripe tomatoes. In any case the tomato paste can be counted on to add a layer of deep, rich tomato flavour.

THIS IS MY GOLD-STANDARD pancake recipe. When I was a country inn chef I tinkered with it every morning. I've tried adding everything under the sun but I always come back to this simple, basic recipe with blueberries. The secret? A preheated skillet.

COUNTRY INN PANCAKES

1 ½ cups (375 mL) of all-purpose flour

1 cup (250 mL) of whole wheat flour

Half a teaspoon of salt

2 tablespoons of brown sugar

1 tablespoon of baking powder

Several large pinches of grated nutmeg

2 eggs

2 sticks of melted butter (8 ounces/250 g)

2 cups (500 mL) of milk

A splash of pure vanilla extract

A cupful or two of blueberries (optional)

SERVES FOUR

Preheat your griddle or skillet over a medium-low heat while you mix the batter.

Whisk both flours, salt, sugar, baking powder and nutmeg together in a large bowl until they're evenly combined. In a separate bowl use the same whisk to beat the eggs, then whisk in the butter, milk and vanilla. Pour the wet mixture into the dry and switch to a wooden spoon. If you're adding blueberries, stir them in and combine with a few quick strokes. Leave the batter a bit lumpy so the flour doesn't overmix and get tough. Let the batter rest for a few minutes; the flour will absorb the milk and the batter will stiffen.

For each batch add a splash of vegetable oil to the pan, then spoon in the batter. Cook until the bottom of each pancake is browned and bubbles break on the top surface. Carefully flip, then cook a few moments more. Drench with butter and maple syrup to start your day with a big smile!

FEEL FREE TO TRY
For a less decadent variation, you can substitute any vegetable oil for the melted butter. For a richer, earthy flavour, replace some or all of the white flour with whole wheat flour. For an apple-pie version, substitute cinnamon for the nutmeg and add a finely diced apple. For a treat, stir in sliced bananas and chocolate chips.

HINTS
Your skillet is perfectly preheated when water drops dance on it without evaporating. Adjust the temperature if the drops evaporate (too hot) or just sit and simmer (too cool). Find that magical sweet spot on your stove.

A WELL-CRAFTED SMOOTHIE tastes so good you'll forget it's good for you! At heart, it's just flavoured fruit purée, so it's easy to make and easy to jazz up with other healthy goodies. It's a great way to jumpstart your day. Gear up your own daily smoothie stand with a menu full of your family's favourite flavours.

POWER SMOOTHIES

Ripe bananas

Frozen blueberries or other frozen berries

Other ripe seasonal fruit, fresh or frozen

Orange, grapefruit, cranberry or apple juice

Yogurt

Honey

Flaxseed oil

Vanilla extract

ORANGE BANANA BERRY

Toss a banana or two into a blender with a handful of frozen berries. Pour in orange juice until it's almost level with the fruit. Add a cupful of yogurt, a splash of flaxseed oil and a dribble of vanilla. Purée until smooth. Drink with a big smile on your face!

BERRY BLASTER

Toss a handful of frozen blueberries into a blender with a handful of frozen strawberries. Pour in enough cranberry or orange juice to almost cover the fruit. Add a cupful of yogurt, a small spoonful of honey, a splash of flaxseed oil and a dribble of vanilla. Purée until smooth. Feel your body sing!

RASPBERRY PEACH

Toss a handful of frozen raspberries into a blender with a handful of peach slices. Pour in enough orange juice to almost submerge the fruit. Add a cupful of yogurt, a splash of flaxseed oil and a dribble of vanilla. Purée until smooth. Mix with champagne for a special brunch treat!

FEEL FREE TO TRY

When bananas get really ripe, they peel easily. Once peeled, toss them in the freezer. Frozen fruit chills and thickens smoothies.

HINTS

I love my immersion blender; it's perfect for quick smoothie jobs and much easier to clean up than my counter blender. A wide-mouth Mason jar makes a great container for puréeing.

Orange, grapefruit and cranberry are the best juice choices. They're not as calorie-rich as apple juice and tend to be higher in nutrients. Active culture yogurt is full of real live goodness; it's a much better choice than sugar-laden substitutes. Bananas add reliable body and smoothness and they're full of nutrients like potassium. Blueberries are packed with antioxidant blood scrubbers that are good for you—even if you don't know what an antioxidant does. Flaxseed oil is loaded with a laundry list of good stuff, including a high concentration of the same omega-3 fatty acids found in fish.

IF TUNA IS THE CHICKEN OF THE SEA, then smoked salmon is the ham. It makes a perfect sandwich. It's a little bit fancy, so it's great for company or a special treat any day of the week. Smokehouses tend to have their own individual styles—some are smokier or sweeter than others—so try a few different versions until you find your favourite!

SMOKED SALMON SANDWICH

A few heaping spoonfuls of cream cheese

A spoonful of mustard

A handful of chopped fresh dill

A squeeze or two of lemon juice

A handful of capers

6 slices of toasted rye bread

4 ounces (125 g) of sliced smoked salmon

A few crisp lettuce leaves

A thinly sliced red onion

MAKES TWO SANDWICHES

Toss the cream cheese, mustard, dill, lemon and capers into a food processor and process them for a few seconds until they're smooth. If you don't have a food processor, soften the cream cheese for a few seconds in the microwave, then mix it with everything in a small bowl.

Spread the cream cheese mixture on two pieces of toasted rye. Top each with a thick layer of smoked salmon, lettuce and red onion. Place one pile on top of the other then top the works with yet another slice of rye. Repeat with the remaining ingredients for the second sandwich. Cut in half—corner-to-corner—and pass around. Enjoy!

FEEL FREE TO TRY
Instead of dill you can chop fresh basil, cilantro or even flat-leaf parsley. If you don't have any capers, try adding a minced pickle.

HINTS
A serrated knife is always best for cutting a thick sandwich. It saws through the layers without dislodging them, unlike a normal blade, which might crush them.

YOU WON'T BELIEVE how richly satisfying a mug of this broth can be or how easy it is to make. Miso is a fermented paste made from soybeans that is a nutritious staple of Japanese and vegetarian cooking. If you can boil water, you can make this broth!

MISO BROTH

Bring the water to a boil in a small pot. Cut any optional vegetables into small pieces so they'll cook quickly. Toss them in with the green onion.

Simmer just long enough for the vegetables to heat through. Turn off the heat and whisk in the miso paste. You won't need to add salt. The miso seasons the broth nicely. Enjoy!

A cup or so of water

A handful of your favourite vegetables

A thinly sliced green onion

A heaping spoonful of miso paste

MAKES ONE STEAMING MUG

FEEL FREE TO TRY

I like simplicity so I usually add just one vegetable to the broth. Some of my favourites are baby spinach, bean sprouts, mushrooms and Asian greens of any kind.

HINTS

Miso is very nutritious and is full of B vitamins. There are many types ranging from light to dark. In general, their flavour gets stronger as they get darker. Some are flavoured with fermented grains. Miso is a bit delicate. Whisk it into the hot water and serve it immediately. The broth can sit for a while but it tastes best freshly made. It's better not to make it in advance and reheat it.

S A L A D S

WANT TO GUARANTEE A HEALTHY MENU and lots of empty plates? A vegetable's best friend is a salad. It's a fast and easy way to fill your table with lots of exciting, healthy flavours. A salad a day will keep the doctor away.

A well-crafted salad is a thing of beauty. Mother Nature's best. Lots of colours. Dancing flavours. Crisp textures. Tasty dressings.

Each of these ten salads is ripe for the picking. Toss them with the dressings that follow, then add your own flavours. Have fun and open your own salad bar!

BOTTOM ROW / LEFT TO RIGHT

BELGIAN ENDIVE SALAD page 47

ARUGULA EGGPLANT SALAD page 48

ASPARAGUS RED ONION SALAD page 49

ROAST POTATO SALAD page 50

SOUTHWESTERN POPCORN SALAD page 51

THIS CLASSIC SALAD has come a long way since its 1924 invention by Caesar Cardini at his Tijuana restaurant. It's now found on virtually every menu in the country—at home and in restaurants. Since there are as many ways to make it as there are cooks, I don't spend a lot of time worrying about authenticity, just flavour. Here's my version.

CAESAR SALAD

42

Half a loaf of Italian bread

A few generous splashes of olive oil

2 heads of romaine lettuce

A thinly sliced red onion

Lemon Parmesan Dressing (page 54)

A sprinkle or two of salt and pepper

SERVES FOUR TO SIX

Preheat your oven to 350°F (180°C). Cut or tear the bread into cubes and toss in a bowl with enough olive oil to lightly coat each one. Spread the cubes in a single layer on a baking sheet and bake until golden brown and crisp, about 15 minutes.

Tear the lettuce into bite-sized pieces and toss with the onion and a half-cup or so of the dressing. Sprinkle the croutons on top and season with salt and pepper.

FEEL FREE TO TRY
Try adding some crumbled bacon to the salad. You can also leave the romaine leaves whole; that's how Caesar Cardini originally did it. For a unique flavour boost, try cutting the whole lettuce head in half lengthwise and grilling it.

HINTS
For an elegant garnish, use a vegetable peeler to shave long slices from a wedge of Parmesan cheese.

BABY SALAD GREENS and tender basil leaves flavour a salad with bright bursts of flavour and a jazzy herb twist. The rest of the salad picks up the theme and runs with it!

ITALIAN BASIL SALAD

Preheat your oven to 350°F (180°C). Cut the bread into cubes and toss with enough olive oil to coat each one. Spread the cubes in a single layer on a baking sheet and bake until golden brown and crisp, about 15 minutes.

Tear or chop the lettuce into bite-sized pieces. Toss it with the basil, onion and a generous splash of the vinaigrette. Top with the croutons and season with salt and pepper.

FEEL FREE TO TRY

There are many salad-green options in today's supermarkets. The sharp, peppery taste of arugula makes a great addition to this salad. Its distinctive kick is as strong as basil.

HINTS

Toss the croutons on top of the salad where they won't get too soggy from the vinaigrette.

Half a loaf of Italian bread

A few generous splashes of olive oil

A 6-ounce (175-g) bag of baby romaine lettuce or any other salad green mixture

A big handful of whole fresh basil leaves

A thinly sliced red onion or the pickled red onions on page 165

Red Wine Herb Vinaigrette (page 54)

A sprinkle or two of salt and pepper

SERVES FOUR TO SIX

THIS IS ONE of my favourite salads! It's loaded with bursts of Asian flavour that give it a ton of fusion character. It tastes exotic but its flavours are still very comfortable.

44

ASIAN SPINACH SALAD

A 6-ounce (175-g) bag of baby spinach leaves

A handful of mint leaves

A few sheets of thinly sliced nori seaweed

A few pieces of thinly sliced candied ginger

Miso Ginger Vinaigrette (page 56)

SERVES FOUR

Toss the spinach, mint, nori and ginger with a generous splash of the dressing. It's as simple as that.

FEEL FREE TO TRY
For a bit of crunch, add some bean sprouts. For sharpness, add thinly sliced red onion. For a garnish, sprinkle on some sesame seeds.

HINTS
Nori is the seaweed used to wrap sushi. It's found in Asian markets and even in most big supermarkets. Check the organic specialty foods section. The easiest way to slice it is with a pair of scissors.

THIS QUICK AND EASY DISH is inspired by a salad common in Thai cooking. Like all Thai food, it's full of nicely balanced flavours. The sweetness of the cucumbers is sharpened by the sourness of the spicy dressing, which in turn is cooled by the refreshing mint.

CUCUMBER MINT SALAD

Thinly slice the cucumber and toss it with the red onion, mint and a generous splash of the dressing. Serve immediately or let rest for a few minutes.

FEEL FREE TO TRY
I often toss crunchy bean sprouts into this salad.

HINTS
When this salad rests the vinegar and sugar in the dressing draw moisture out of the cucumber. It turns a bit watery and softens. That's okay; it still tastes great. Just toss again before serving.

A large cucumber

A thinly sliced red onion

A handful of mint leaves

Spicy Asian Dressing (page 56)

SERVES FOUR TO SIX

FENNEL IS ONE OF my favourite vegetables and this dish really shows off its crisp sweetness and subtle licorice flavours. Try it. Its simplicity will blow you away! It'll soon become one of your favourites.

FENNEL SALAD

A fennel bulb

The juice and zest from half a lemon

A spoonful of honey

A few splashes of olive oil

A sprinkle or two of salt and pepper

SERVES TWO TO FOUR

Remove the stalks from the top of the fennel bulb. Cut the head in half through the core. Carefully trim out the woody core, then slice the remaining bulb as thinly as possible. Alternatively, shred it through the large holes of a box grater.

Whisk the lemon, honey, olive oil and seasoning together in a nice salad bowl. Toss with the fennel, then grab some forks!

FEEL FREE TO TRY
For lots of fresh herb flavour, toss a handful of cool mint leaves, sliced chives or aromatic basil leaves into the salad.

HINTS
Specialty kitchen stores sell a fancy French slicing tool known as a mandoline. With it the pros can slice the fennel paper-thin—and do other amazing things with onions and potatoes. It's nice to have one but if you don't—no worries—the salad still tastes awesome!

BELGIAN ENDIVE IS a vegetable that's often overlooked in the produce section. Its crisp texture and balanced sweet and bitter flavours make it a great choice for any salad. This one is a great way to show off the bright flavours of the vanilla vinaigrette.

BELGIAN ENDIVE SALAD
WITH VANILLA AND RAISINS

Toss the endive and raisins with a splash of the vinaigrette and the seasonings. Couldn't be easier.

FEEL FREE TO TRY

Toss in some sliced almonds for a bit of crunchy, nutty texture. You can soften dry chewy raisins by tossing them with a few drops of water then covering with plastic wrap and microwaving them for 20 or 30 seconds. Let them stand for a minute or two and they'll soften nicely.

HINTS

When you choose endive look for firm, pure white heads with light green tips; if the heads have brown spots or the tips are yellow, they're past their prime.

4 heads of thinly sliced
Belgian endive

A cupful of plump raisins

Vanilla Vinaigrette (page 57)

A sprinkle or two of salt
and pepper

SERVES FOUR

SHARP, PEPPERY ARUGULA meets rich, buttery eggplant and vibrant roasted tomatoes in this wonderful salad. This group of flavours was always a favourite for my restaurant guests and is now a regular on the menu at home.

ARUGULA EGGPLANT SALAD

48

A large eggplant

A few splashes of olive oil

A sprinkle or two of salt and pepper

A few large handfuls of arugula

A handful of Oven-Dried Tomatoes (page 162)

Balsamic Vinaigrette (page 57)

SERVES FOUR

Preheat your oven to 400°F (200°C). Cut the eggplant into 8 or 9 thick slices. Lay them on a baking pan and generously brush each one with olive oil. Lightly season them with salt and pepper and bake until they begin to turn golden brown, about 20 minutes. Let them rest until they're cool enough to handle, then cut each into quarters.

Toss the eggplant with the arugula, tomatoes and a generous splash of the vinaigrette.

FEEL FREE TO TRY
For lots of bright herb flavour, toss a handful of whole fresh basil leaves into the salad.

HINTS
Keep an eye on the eggplant as it roasts. When it turns opaque and just starts to brown, its texture becomes wonderfully smooth. That's the best time to pull it from the oven.

ASPARAGUS IS GABE'S favourite vegetable so I've invented a lot of ways to serve it to keep him from getting bored. Here it stars in a tasty salad that grown-ups will love too!

ASPARAGUS RED ONION SALAD

Trim off and discard the tough woody bottoms of the asparagus spears. Cut the spears into two pieces. Steam them until they're bright green and tender—but not mushy. Immediately run them under cold water to stop them from cooking further. Drain well.

Toss the asparagus with the remaining ingredients and enjoy!

FEEL FREE TO TRY

If you don't have any pickled red onions, just toss in some thinly sliced raw red onion.

HINTS

Steaming the asparagus over simmering water preserves the flavour, colour and nutrients that would be lost if it was boiled in the same water. If you're prepping this salad in advance, wait until the last second to add the lemon; that way its acidic juice won't dull the bright green colour of the asparagus.

2 large bunches of asparagus

The juice and zest of a lemon

A generous splash of extra virgin olive oil

A handful of fresh dill

Pickled Red Onions (page 165)

A sprinkle or two of salt and pepper

SERVES FOUR

ROASTING ADDS FLAVOUR to just about anything—including mellow potatoes headed for a salad. The sharp flavours of capers, mustard and vinegar really perk them up. This is a popular dish at my family's summer beach picnics, but it's great in the middle of winter too!

ROAST POTATO SALAD

4 or 5 thick bacon slices

20 or so baby red potatoes or other baby potatoes

A sprinkle or two of salt and pepper

A handful of flat-leaf parsley leaves

A few heaping spoonfuls of capers

A big spoonful of grainy mustard

A splash of red wine vinegar

SERVES FOUR

Stack the bacon slices on top of each other and cut crosswise into thin pieces. Toss them into a large sauté pan, add a splash of water and begin heating the works over medium-high heat. When the water evaporates and the bacon begins to brown, turn the heat down a notch and continue cooking until it's all nice and crisp. Strain and reserve the fat.

Meanwhile, preheat your oven to 400°F (200°C). Cut the potatoes in half. Toss them with the bacon fat and salt and pepper, then roast them until they're golden brown, about 40 minutes. Cool to room temperature.

Toss the potatoes with the remaining ingredients. Serve right away or refrigerate and save for later. This salad is great when it's made the night before the party!

FEEL FREE TO TRY

If you don't have capers, try mincing up a pickle or two. And try using a big handful of fresh dill fronds along with the parsley leaves.

HINTS

By adding water to the raw bacon you're less likely to burn it, as it gradually releases its fat and browns evenly.

WHO SAYS POPCORN is just for snacks? It plays a starring role in this simple, tasty salad along with some of the other vibrant flavours of the Southwest—where popcorn was invented. It's fun to eat, the popcorn tastes great and, since it's a whole grain, it's good for you!

SOUTHWESTERN POPCORN SALAD

Toss the popcorn with the cumin powder, salt, pepper and olive oil. Toss with the greens, cilantro, red pepper and a generous splash of the dressing. Grab a fork and have fun!

FEEL FREE TO TRY

If you'd like, replace the popcorn with grilled corn. Rub a few ears with oil and grill them until golden brown. Shave the grilled kernels off the cob.

HINTS

It's easier to evenly spread the cumin powder and seasoning throughout the salad by tossing it with the popcorn first. Otherwise you might bite into little pockets of it in the salad leaves.

A few handfuls of unseasoned popcorn

A pinch of ground cumin powder

A sprinkle or two of salt and pepper

A splash of olive oil

3 or 4 large handfuls of any mixed baby greens

A handful of fresh cilantro leaves

A thinly sliced red bell pepper

Honey Lime Dressing (page 55)

SERVES FOUR

DRESSINGS

IF A VEGETABLE'S BEST FRIEND is a salad, then a salad's best friend is a tasty dressing! Easy to add, healthy flavour. Simple. Start with one part vinegar, or anything sour like lemons or limes. Then add three parts of everything else—oils, cheese, honey, miso paste or whatever. Somehow the tastes and flavours always seem to balance!

These recipes fill a standard Mason jar so you'll have plenty of leftovers. Make them once and enjoy many different salads! The leftovers should be refrigerated. If they firm up just spoon into a salad bowl and whisk until they soften. You can also cut the recipes in half or even double them and give some away.

With each of these dressings, mix everything together until a smooth dressing forms. A blender, food processor or an old-fashioned whisk and bowl all work well, but I prefer my immersion blender. It's easier to clean up!

IF YOU ORDER A CAESAR SALAD at my house, this is how I'll dress it up. It's full of classic flavours and great with crisp romaine lettuce and crunchy croutons. It also makes a great all-purpose toss for any other salad on the menu!

LEMON PARMESAN DRESSING

A cupful of extra virgin olive oil

The juice and zest of 2 lemons

A few dashes of Worcestershire sauce

A heaping spoonful of Dijon mustard

Half a cup or so of grated Parmesan cheese

A few cloves of chopped garlic

A sprinkle or two of salt and pepper

MAKES ABOUT 2 CUPFULS

FEEL FREE TO TRY

For more authentic Caesar flavour add a few anchovies or a generous squeeze of anchovy paste. If you don't like the pungency of raw garlic, but love garlic flavour, try adding a head of roast garlic. If you have some leftover bacon fat, add a spoonful for intense—but naughty—bacon flavour; it's an old short-order cook's trick!

HINTS

For best results use a top-notch Parmesan cheese like Grana Padano or even a strongly flavoured Romano cheese.

THIS CLASSIC GROUP of flavours is often called Italian dressing. A few days rest after mixing will allow the dried herbs to come to life. Like many things in life it gets better as it ages!

RED WINE HERB VINAIGRETTE

Half a cup or so of red wine vinegar

A cupful of extra virgin olive oil

2 heaping spoonfuls of Dijon mustard

Several heaping spoonfuls of grated Romano cheese

A generous spoonful of dried oregano

A generous spoonful of dried basil

A sprinkle or two of salt and pepper

MAKES ABOUT 2 CUPFULS

FEEL FREE TO TRY

For lots more fresh herb flavour, add minced fresh rosemary or thyme. You can use pecorino or Parmesan cheese rather than the Romano.

HINTS

Mustard contains lecithin, which encourages oil and watery liquids like vinegar to combine into a smooth vinaigrette.

THIS BRIGHTLY FLAVOURED DRESSING will add tropical flavour to your favourite greens. The sharpness of the lime balances the sweetness of the honey, and their citrus and floral fragrances blend beautifully!

HONEY LIME DRESSING

FEEL FREE TO TRY

For another citrus flavour, replace the 4 limes with 2 lemons. Try tossing some mandarin orange segments or shredded coconut into the salad too. A handful of chopped mint adds a nice touch.

HINTS

Zesting releases an intensely aromatic oil in the skin of citrus fruit. It's a flavour burst too good to pass up!

The juice and zest of 4 limes

A few heaping spoonfuls of honey

A spoonful of mustard

A cupful of olive oil

A sprinkle or two of salt and pepper

MAKES ABOUT 2 CUPS OR SO

I LOVE THE FLAVOURS of Japan; they add distinctive flair to any salad. Balance the earthy goodness of miso with aromatic ginger, sharp rice wine vinegar and floral honey.

MISO GINGER VINAIGRETTE

Half a cup or so of rice wine vinegar

A cupful of any vegetable oil

A few heaping spoonfuls of honey

A heaping spoonful or two of miso paste

A small knob of grated ginger

A few dashes of toasted sesame oil

A few dashes of soy sauce

MAKES ABOUT 2 CUPS

FEEL FREE TO TRY

You can substitute white wine vinegar for the rice wine vinegar. Sesame oil is very strong—a little bit of its toasty flavour goes a long way. For maximum sesame punch, drop the ginger, add a touch more sesame oil and rename the works Miso Sesame Vinaigrette!

HINTS

The rich, full-bodied roundness of miso makes this an ideal marinade or dressing.

THIS BRIGHTLY FLAVOURED dressing doesn't include any oil and is most often used for flavouring vegetables, not greens. For a spicy treat, toss some with bean sprouts, sliced cucumbers and sliced red onions. I also love it as a quick marinade for grilling fish.

SPICY ASIAN DRESSING

A cup or so of rice wine vinegar

2 heaping spoonfuls of Thai chili garlic sauce

2 heaping spoonfuls of sugar

A sprinkle or two of salt

MAKES MORE THAN A CUPFUL

FEEL FREE TO TRY

You can replace some or all of the vinegar with lime juice. For more Asian flavour, add a touch of toasted sesame oil.

HINTS

There are many types of chili sauces, each unique. I particularly like Thailand's—it's a mildly spicy blend of chili peppers and garlic known as sambal. You can use it anywhere you'd use slightly spicier Tabasco sauce.

IT MAY SEEM ODD to flavour a vinaigrette with vanilla, but once you try it you'll know why it works so well. Vanilla mellows the sharpness of vinegar with a clean, crisp edge that's very refreshing. It's a great way to dress up simple mixed greens.

VANILLA VINAIGRETTE

FEEL FREE TO TRY

For more flavour contrast, try substituting sherry balsamic vinegar for the neutral white wine vinegar.

HINTS

Aromatic vanilla is not just for dessert! Its flavour dominates this dressing, so this is a great place to show off your best pure extract. If you're feeling really extravagant, finely mince in a whole vanilla bean.

A cupful of extra virgin olive oil

Half a cup or so of white wine vinegar

2 spoonfuls of honey

A spoonful or two of pure vanilla extract

A spoonful of Dijon mustard

A sprinkle or two of salt and pepper

MAKES ALMOST 2 CUPS

BALSAMIC VINEGAR IS PACKED with flavour. Since it's actually more sweet than sour, it adds just a touch of edge to this dressing. Its wonderful woody scent and the subtle licorice aromas of the fennel seeds are an exotic blend that will brighten any salad.

BALSAMIC VINAIGRETTE

Briefly pulse the fennel seeds in a coffee grinder, spice grinder or food processor. Don't turn them into a powder; leave them a bit rustic.

Then mix everything together until smooth.

FEEL FREE TO TRY

For stronger balsamic flavour, try concentrating the vinegar. Simmer a full cup until it is reduced by half, then mix away.

HINTS

Balsamic vinegar's distinctive flavour comes from long aging in wooden barrels. The best bottles are 50 or more years old and get to be quite expensive. Look for the word 'traditional' on the label to be sure you're getting your money's worth.

A few heaping spoonfuls of fennel seeds

A cupful of extra virgin olive oil

Half a cup or so of balsamic vinegar

Half a cup or so of honey

A heaping spoonful of Dijon mustard

A sprinkle or two of salt and pepper

MAKES ABOUT 2 CUPS OR SO

THE SHARP MUSKY FLAVOURS of sherry vinegar are a perfect match for the sweet woodiness of maple syrup. Together, they flavour a great all-purpose dressing for any day of the week. In my house I serve this dressing so often that our friends call it the house dressing!

58

SHERRY MAPLE VINAIGRETTE

Half a cup or so of sherry vinegar

Half a cup or so of maple syrup

A cupful of extra virgin olive oil

A spoonful of Dijon mustard

A sprinkle or two of salt and pepper

MAKES ABOUT 2 CUPS OR SO

FEEL FREE TO TRY

For another fruity flavour, try apple cider vinegar instead of sherry.

HINTS

Maple syrup is about the same consistency as olive oil so they combine well. Together they make this dressing extra smooth!

IF YOU LIKE THE STRONG flavour of goat's cheese, this vinaigrette's for you. Its distinctive pungent taste complements the sweet honey and sharp vinegar. I know it's a grown-up flavour but my son loves it!

GOAT'S CHEESE VINAIGRETTE

FEEL FREE TO TRY

The strong flavour of goat's cheese combines well with other strong ingredients. I often use ground caraway seed, ground cumin seed or minced rosemary. Try a dash of hot sauce to balance it. You can replace some or all of the vinegar with lemon juice for a citrus edge.

HINTS

Oil and vinegar normally avoid each other, but the thick and creamy goat's cheese helps bring them together.

A quarter cup or so of white wine vinegar

Half a cup or so of your best olive oil

An overflowing spoonful of honey

Half a cup or so of goat's cheese

A sprinkle or two of salt and pepper

MAKES MORE THAN A CUPFUL

THE WHOLE PURÉED TOMATO in this dressing is guaranteed to add garden flavour to any salad! The thick purée holds the aromatic olive oil and bright lemon in a smooth embrace. Use a ripe tomato and it'll taste like a summer day!

TOMATO LEMON DRESSING

After blending all the ingredients together, strain through the finest strainer you have. This will remove seeds and tiny bits of tomato skin. But don't worry if you don't have a strainer, it'll still taste great!

A large ripe tomato

The juice and zest of a whole lemon

Half a cup or so of your best olive oil

A sprinkle or two of salt and pepper

MAKES MORE THAN A CUPFUL

FEEL FREE TO TRY

If you like the sharp pungency of garlic, toss in a few cloves for extra flavour. To brighten out-of-season tomatoes add a spoonful of tomato paste.

HINTS

If you can't find a truly ripe tomato, use a few canned ones. They have lots of sunny flavour because they're picked ripe in the field just before processing. Very often they have more flavour than fresh ones that have to be picked green so they can survive the trip to your house.

D I N N E R S

THESE ARE DISHES YOU CAN BUILD your daily life around. In my home they anchor the ritual of my family's evening meal. Real flavours. Healthy choices. Empty plates. Some are weekend fancy, when we have more time on our hands. Some are school-night plain and simple. Some need bowls, others just plates. All will have your family asking for seconds and your co-workers asking for the recipe when you take the leftovers to lunch.

They're easy to cook, too. They use simple tools, familiar ingredients and usually just one pot. Does your house have a dishwasher on staff? Mine doesn't! And these dishes aren't expensive. Isn't it nice when you don't have to mortgage the stove to afford a nice dinner?

Pick a recipe and change it. Evolve it. Experiment. Go wild. You'll feel like you're in cooking school! Each dinner suggests other complementary dishes in this book. Together they'll form an entire meal for your family. Of course, you're free to pick and choose your own!

INEXPENSIVE BLADE STEAK plays the starring role in this easy to make, one-pot meal. Braising transforms this simmering steak into a richly flavoured, Asian-inspired stew. My family loves it. It's a stew and a salad in the same bowl!

62

ORANGE GINGER BEEF

A splash of vegetable oil

A sprinkle or two of salt and pepper

A boneless flank steak, about 1 pound (500 g)

A few chopped onions

A small knob of unpeeled ginger, thinly sliced

A 10-ounce (284-mL) can of beef stock

A cup or so of orange juice

A cup or so of orange marmalade

A generous splash of soy sauce

A spoonful of five-spice powder

Another sprinkle or two of salt and pepper

A 10-ounce (300-g) bag of baby spinach

A handful of bean sprouts

1 bunch of chopped green onions

A handful of cilantro leaves

SERVES FOUR

Preheat a large pot over a medium-high heat, then splash in enough oil to thinly coat the bottom. Season the steak and sear until it's evenly browned on both sides. Remove the meat and set aside for a moment.

Add the onions and ginger to the pan and stir for a few minutes until they lightly brown. If the pan starts to burn, add a splash of water and continue.

Return the meat to the pot and add the beef stock, orange juice, marmalade, soy sauce and five-spice powder. Bring the works to a simmer, then reduce the heat to the lowest setting that will maintain the simmer. Place a tight-fitting lid on the pot to contain the tenderizing steam. Continue simmering until the meat is tender enough to break into smaller pieces, about 1 to 1 ½ hours. Taste and season the broth.

Divide the spinach and bean sprouts evenly between four bowls. Stir the green onions and cilantro leaves into the stew—reserving a few—then ladle over the veggies. Top with a sprinkling of the reserved cilantro and enjoy!

FEEL FREE TO TRY
Cilantro roots have lots of flavour. If some are still attached to your bunch, add them to the stew. Rinse them well, chop them finely, and stir them in while the stew simmers. They're loaded with cilantro flavour and can handle more heat than the delicate leaves!

HINTS
Searing the meat adds lots of rich caramelized flavours to the stew. Ginger skin doesn't always have to be peeled—just rinsed. The flesh doesn't always have to be grated either. When it simmers it tenderizes nicely.

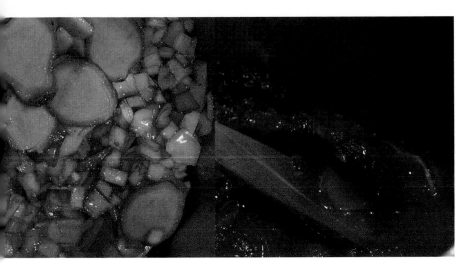

GOES WELL WITH . . .

GOES WELL WITH . . .

BRAISED LEEKS page 127

CAESAR SALAD page 42

POTATO BACON CHEDDAR TART page 109

A THICK CRUSTY STEAK is a rare luxury for me, so when it's on the menu I like it to be special. Earthy mushrooms and sharp tarragon add just the right flavours to jazz it up. With a glass of red wine in hand I feel like I'm sitting in my favourite steakhouse!

PAN ROAST STEAK
WITH TARRAGON MUSHROOM SAUCE

Toss a dab of the butter into a sauté pan, then add the onion and mushrooms. Sauté over medium-high heat until the moisture released by the veggies simmers away and they begin to brown, about 10 minutes. Add a splash of sherry and continue cooking until the liquid reduces again. Add a splash or two of cream and the tarragon and simmer just until it reduces enough to form a sauce. Season with salt and pepper.

Meanwhile, season the steaks generously with lots of salt and pepper. Melt another dab of butter with a splash of oil in a thick-bottomed fry pan set over medium-high heat. (Butter burns at a much lower temperature than oil.) By mixing the two you'll get the best of both worlds: a butter-flavoured oil that won't burn. When the butter begins to sizzle add the steaks and begin searing them.

Cook the first side of the steaks until they're beautifully caramelized, about 5 or 6 minutes. Flip them over and cook on the other side until they're medium-rare, another 8 to 10 minutes or so. Continue flipping until they're cooked the way you like them. To tell the meat's doneness, do what all chefs have done when they were apprentices: cut a small slit in one side and peek at the centre.

Toss the tarragon in the sauce. Top the steaks with the tarragon mushroom sauce and enjoy!

A few dabs of butter

A minced onion

A few handfuls of sliced mushrooms

A big splash of sherry

A generous splash or two of cream

1 small bunch of chopped fresh tarragon

Lots of salt and pepper

Four 6-ounce (175-g) striploin or sirloin steaks

A splash of vegetable oil

SERVES FOUR

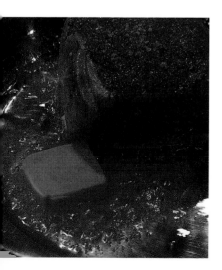

FEEL FREE TO TRY
Any mushroom—not just buttons—will flavour this sauce. Try shiitakes, oysters or portabellos. Also try replacing the tarragon with other strong, fresh herbs, like rosemary or thyme.

HINTS
Seasoning the steaks before you cook them encourages the meat to release a bit of surface moisture that will help them brown nicely. Don't overload your pan; too much meat will keep the temperature too low for proper browning. Ask your butcher to cut the meat into thick cubes instead of thin steaks; they'll cook more evenly and you'll be able to fit more in the pan.

I LOVE THE WAY stewing transforms inexpensive, tough cuts of beef into tasty, tender stew. The earthy flavours of root vegetables combine with full-bodied beef stock and aromatic red wine to form a rich flavour base. The only thing better than a bowl full of hearty stew is the same bowl with a biscuit topping!

BISCUIT-CRUSTED BEEF STEW

2 pounds (1 kg) or so of stew beef

A sprinkle or two of salt and pepper

A splash of vegetable oil

A few carrots, peeled and roughly chopped

A few stalks of celery, roughly chopped

A few potatoes, peeled and roughly chopped

A few parsnips, peeled and roughly chopped

A few onions, peeled and roughly chopped

A turnip, peeled and roughly chopped

A small can of tomato paste

A jar of pickled baby white onions

Half a bottle or so of hearty red wine

2 or 3 cups (500–750 mL) of home-made or canned beef stock

A few bay leaves

A few sprigs of fresh rosemary

Half the recipe for Frozen Butter Biscuits (page 134)

A few handfuls of frozen peas

SERVES SIX TO EIGHT
WITH LEFTOVERS

Preheat a large, thick-bottomed pot over medium-high heat. Meanwhile, pat the beef dry with a paper towel. Cut it into large cubes, if not already cubed, and season it. Add a few splashes of oil to the pot—enough to cover the bottom in a thin layer—then toss in enough meat to form a single sizzling layer. Sear the meat on every side until it's evenly browned. As it browns, remove it from the pan, adding more meat and oil as needed. Once the meat is done discard the remaining oil—but keep all the browned bits in the pan. They'll add lots of flavour!

Add half of the vegetables—reserving the other half—and all the meat to the pot. Add the tomato paste, baby onions and enough wine and beef stock to just barely cover the works. Add the bay leaves and rosemary and bring the pot to a simmer. Continue cooking until the meat is almost tender, about an hour, then add the remaining vegetables. I add them in two batches: the first dissolves into the stew and thickens it, while the second retains its shape, colour and texture. Continue simmering until the meat and veggies are tender, about another 30 minutes.

Meanwhile, prepare a batch of your favourite biscuit dough or a half-batch of my frozen butter biscuit dough. Preheat the oven to 400°F (200°C). When the stew is tender season it, then stir in the peas and ladle it into several oven-proof bowls. Fit a piece of biscuit dough onto each bowl. Place them on a tray to catch any drips. Bake until the biscuit toppings are nicely browned, about 20 minutes.

FEEL FREE TO TRY

Use any combination of root vegetables you have on hand. You can choose to add the biscuit crust to one big dish of the stew instead of several individual ones. When I'm making biscuits for beef stew I substitute whole wheat flour for half of the white flour, for a richer flavour.

HINTS

Be patient when you're browning the meat; it takes a little time. The caramelized flavours are the secret to a rich hearty stew. You can use any cut of beef that's labelled for stewing, simmering or braising. Try not to make the biscuit topping too thick or the bottom of it won't cook—an inch or so is about right.

GOES WELL WITH . . .

CAESAR SALAD page 42

GARLIC-STEAMED BROCCOLI page 122

ZUCCHINI WITH TOMATOES page 121
AND OREGANO

THE SUNNY FLAVOURS of the Mediterranean and the aroma of a live wood fire in my backyard make this one of my favourite ways to serve lamb. It's a great excuse to fire up your grill—any kind of grill, any time of year. Both the marinade and the tapenade are wonderful with all meats and fish.

GRILLED LEG OF LAMB
WITH TOMATO MINT TAPENADE

68

FOR THE LAMB

A boneless leg of lamb

A cupful of olive oil

A few heaping spoonfuls of dried oregano

6 or 8 minced garlic cloves

The zest and juice of 2 lemons

Several heaping spoonfuls of any mustard (I prefer grainy)

A sprinkle or two of salt and pepper

FOR THE TAPENADE

A handful of dried tomatoes

A handful of pitted calamata olives

A few anchovies

The juice and zest of a lemon

1 or 2 minced garlic cloves

A generous splash of extra virgin olive oil

A handful of mint leaves

A few heaping spoonfuls of capers

SERVES SIX, WITH LEFTOVERS

Open the lamb up into one large piece by cutting through the centre hole where the bone was removed. It's okay if you end up with two pieces. Because the meat is now thinner it will be easier to grill. Vigorously whisk the oil, oregano, garlic, lemon, mustard, salt and pepper together until a smooth marinade forms. Place the lamb in a dish that's just big enough to hold it, add the marinade and rub it all over the meat. Cover the bowl with plastic wrap and marinate in the refrigerator for at least an hour; for maximum flavour marinate it overnight and turn it a few times.

Toss all the tapenade ingredients—except the capers—into your food processor and purée well. Stir in the capers last so they keep their shape.

Preheat your grill to its highest setting. For medium-rare, grill the lamb for 10 minutes or so on the first side, then another 5 to 10 minutes on the other side. To check the doneness, feel free to cut a small slit into the thickest part and have a peek! Before you slice the meat let it rest on a rack for at least 10 minutes. Serve with the tapenade and enjoy all the sunny flavours!

FEEL FREE TO TRY

If you don't have a grill you can simply roast the lamb at 400°F (200°C) for 30 to 40 minutes or so. A tapenade is a Mediterranean condiment traditionally made from olives and capers. If you don't like anchovies, leave them out!

HINTS

Searing meat does not seal in its juices. That's a myth. Instead, it flavours the meat. Heat stresses the meat; resting it for a few minutes allows the fibres to relax so that when you slice you don't lose any juice. For best results, use a cooling rack; a plate works too, but you'll lose a bit of juice where it touches the meat.

GOES WELL WITH . . .

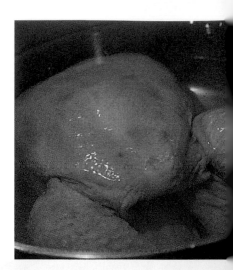

GOES WELL WITH . . .

ITALIAN BASIL SALAD page 43

GARLIC STEAMED BROCCOLI page 122

ASIAN SPINACH SALAD page 44

BRINING, ONE OF THE OLDEST techniques in the world, is a very common way to preserve food with salt. In today's kitchen, it's an amazingly simple way to make the juiciest chicken you've ever had! I love how the vegetable base in this recipe soaks up all the flavour of the roasting chicken.

BRINED ROAST CHICKEN

Whisk the salt and sugar into the water until they're completely dissolved. Place the chicken in a large, non-reactive bowl or pot and completely cover it with the water. Refrigerate it in the brine for 2 hours. Remove it, rinse it and pat it dry with a clean towel.

Preheat your oven to 350°F (180°C). Toss the vegetables with the oil and a bit of salt and pepper, then pour them into a casserole dish or shallow roasting pan. Sit the chicken on top and roast it until an instant-read meat thermometer registers 160°F (70°C) in the thickest part of the breast and 165°F (74°C) in the thigh. This will take about 90 minutes.

As soon as the chicken is cool enough to handle—and without taking it out of the pan—cut off the legs and slice off the breasts. Cut as much of the meat as possible off the bones and serve with the vegetables and all the yummy juices.

8 cups (2 L) of water

½ cup (125 mL) of salt

½ cup (125 mL) of sugar

A fresh chicken

1 or 2 chopped onions

A few chopped parsnips

A few chopped carrots

A few stalks of chopped celery

A splash of olive oil

A sprinkle or two of salt and pepper

SERVES FOUR TO SIX

FEEL FREE TO TRY

You can flavour the vegetables with any fresh herb you care to. Try mincing some fresh rosemary, thyme or sage and tossing it in before you begin roasting. For a flavour boost toss a handful of chopped parsley or even sliced basil with the vegetables after you've cut all the meat off the bones.

HINTS

The salt in the brine encourages the chicken flesh to absorb the water and retain it within its cells. The result is a noticeably juicier chicken but not a saltier one. Toss the leftover carcass into a small pot and cover it with water, simmer for an hour or two and you'll have a tasty chicken broth!

VANILLA ACCENTS SAVOURY flavours just as well as it emphasizes sweet ones. In this simple braised dish its mysterious presence highlights the woodsy aroma of the rosemary. Chicken thighs are flavour sponges and they easily show off the results.

ROSEMARY VANILLA CHICKEN

8 chicken thighs

A generous splash of vegetable oil

A sprinkle or two of salt and pepper

2 sliced onions

2 chopped carrots

A few cupfuls of chicken broth

Half a bottle of your favourite Chardonnay

A plump vanilla bean, minced, or a spoonful of vanilla extract

The needles from two large sprigs of fresh rosemary

SERVES FOUR

Remove the bones from the chicken by slitting the back of each thigh with a sharp knife and cutting around the bone. Carefully trim the meat off each bone. Try to leave the thigh in one piece, but it's okay if it ends up in several pieces. Don't toss the bones away.

Preheat a large frying pan over medium-high heat and splash in enough oil to lightly coat the bottom. Season the chicken meat with salt and pepper, then sear it, along with the bones, until golden brown on every side. This is the best opportunity to add the rich flavours of caramelization. Remove the meat and bones and set aside. Pour off most of the accumulated fat, then add the onions and carrots to the hot pan. Sauté them for a few minutes until they soften slightly and their flavours brighten. Stir to loosen any brown bits adhering to the bottom of the pan. These caramelized juices from the meat will add a ton of flavour to the dish.

Add the chicken meat and bones back to the pan. Pour in the chicken broth and wine, reserving a sip for you of course! Add the vanilla and rosemary. Bring everything to a simmer and adjust the heat to the lowest setting that will maintain the simmer. Place a tight-fitting lid on the pan to capture evaporating moisture and braise on the stovetop until the thighs are tender, about 45 minutes. Fish out the bones and toss them; they've done their job and added lots of flavour. Remove the thighs and rest them for a minute. Turn up the heat and reduce the liquid by half until it thickens into a sauce. Return the chicken to the sauce, taste, then season as needed with a little more salt and pepper. Enjoy!

FEEL FREE TO TRY
Braised chicken can be flavoured in many different ways, so try experimenting with other herbs or spices, red wine or fruit juices.

HINTS
If the chicken sticks to the pan while you're browning it, be patient. It will shrink slightly as it browns and eventually release easily from the pan.

To save time you can leave the bones in the chicken and simply remove them as you dine.

GOES WELL WITH . . .

ASPARAGUS RED ONION SALAD page 49

BROWN BUTTER MASHED POTATOES page 106

BROWN RICE AND LENTILS page 115

GOES WELL WITH . . .

GRILLED VEGETABLE SKEWERS page 111

FENNEL SALAD page 46

CORN POLENTA page 119

THIS IS ONE OF the tastiest ways ever invented to flavour grilled chicken—jerk marinade. I love its Caribbean allspice flavour and the smoke and medium heat this version picks up from the chipotle pepper. The marinade is essentially highly seasoned, puréed, raw onion, and the longer the chicken sits in it the better it tastes!

JERK CHICKEN

Cut the chicken into 8 pieces. First, remove the legs and separate them into drumsticks and thighs. Remove the breasts by gently slicing along the centre breastbone and then along the rib cage, under the breast meat. Cut each in half. Trim off and discard any loose flaps of skin. Freeze the remaining carcass for your next broth.

Toss the onions, lime, molasses, oil, allspice, chipotle pepper and salt into a blender and purée until a smooth paste forms. Scrape it into a large bowl, add the chicken pieces and toss until thoroughly coated. Wrap with plastic wrap or place in freezer bags and marinate in the refrigerator for at least 2 hours and preferably overnight.

Preheat your grill or barbecue to medium-high. When it's hot, toss on the chicken pieces, skin side down. Turn them after 10 to 15 minutes or so and continue cooking the other side for another 10 to 15 minutes or so, until done. The breasts usually finish ahead of the legs and thighs.

A 2-pound (1-kg) chicken

2 bunches of roughly chopped green onions, about a dozen in total, with the root ends trimmed off

The juice and zest of 4 limes

2 or 3 heaping spoonfuls of molasses

A splash of vegetable oil

A spoonful of ground allspice

A chipotle pepper, dried or in adobe sauce

A few sprinkles of salt

SERVES FOUR

FEEL FREE TO TRY
You can substitute any individual cut of chicken for the whole chicken. You can also use your favourite chili pepper or hot sauce in place of the chipotle pepper. Molasses adds rich, traditional flavour but if you don't have any—or you'd prefer a lighter flavour—substitute honey.

HINTS
Because there's a touch of sugar in the marinade, grilling at the highest setting would burn the chicken. A slower, more patient heat is the key! If the grill flares up and the chicken begins to char, splash on some water until the flames subside. To check it for doneness, simply cut a piece and have a peek!

GOES WELL WITH . . .

SOUTHWESTERN POPCORN SALAD page 51

ROASTED GARLIC BREAD page 133

GRILLED VEGETABLE SKEWERS page 111

THE FLAVOURS OF THE SOUTHWEST shine in this unique soup. It's thickened with cornmeal, which reflects the traditional use of corn tortillas to add body to Mexican broths. My family loves its pleasing spiciness and hearty goodness. It tastes like a sunny day in Mexico!

SOUTHWESTERN CHICKEN CORN SOUP

Preheat your grill to its highest setting. Toss the corn and pepper halves with a splash of vegetable oil and lots of salt and pepper. Place on the grill, putting the peppers skin side down. Grill until the vegetables start to char and become tender, about 10 minutes. Remove the corn from the grill and place the peppers in a small bowl. Cover with plastic wrap, which will allow the steam to loosen the skins. After 10 minutes or so the charred skin will be easy to peel off. Thinly slice the peppers and set them aside to add to the finished soup. When the corn is cool, cut off the kernels and set aside.

Heat a splash of oil in a heavy-bottomed soup pot over medium-high heat. Add the onions and cook, stirring frequently, until they turn golden brown. After a few minutes the onions will lose their pungency and actually taste quite bland; once they begin to brown their flavour will revive. Add the garlic and cumin powder. Stir for a few moments longer until they are heated through. (Adding the garlic at this stage prevents it from scorching; it burns much faster than onion. The heat also brightens the cumin's flavour.) Add the chicken broth and chili pepper, then slowly stir in the cornmeal. Continue stirring as the granules swell and thicken the liquid, about 10 minutes. Stir in the chicken meat and simmer for a few minutes more until it cooks through.

Stir in the reserved corn kernels and red pepper strips, grated cheese, lime and cilantro. Fish out the chili pepper, mince it and toss it back in. Taste, and season as needed with a bit more salt. Garnish with a few more sprigs of cilantro and a dollop of sour cream if you like. Enjoy!

FEEL FREE TO TRY
Grilling the veggies is an optional step. Instead you can choose to use a can of creamed corn and sauté the chopped pepper with the onions. You can also roast the corn and peppers under the broiler in your oven.

HINTS
If you're worried about the heat of the chili pepper, you have the option of removing it when the broth reaches the heat level you prefer. After you've added the pepper to the broth, taste it every few minutes until you like the spiciness.

4 ears of husked corn

2 red bell peppers, halved, and seeds and stem discarded

A few splashes of vegetable oil

Lots of salt and pepper

2 or 3 thinly sliced onions

2 or 3 minced garlic cloves

A spoonful of cumin powder

8 cups (2 L) of home-made or canned chicken broth

A jalapeño, ancho, or poblano chili pepper, halved, and seeds and stem discarded

A cupful of fine cornmeal

2 thinly sliced chicken breasts

A cup or so of grated aged cheddar cheese

The juice and zest of 1 lime

1 bunch of chopped cilantro

A few sprinkles of salt

A few spoonfuls of sour cream (optional)

SERVES FOUR TO SIX

THE SWEET AND SOUR FLAVOUR of apples is the perfect way to jazz up the relatively bland flavour of pork. Braising them together gives the often-overlooked shoulder cut a melt-in-the-mouth tenderness. A shot of mustard jazzes up the works. Don't count on leftovers!

APPLE BRAISED PORK

A splash of vegetable oil

A 2-pound (1-kg) or so pork shoulder roast, cut in half

2 or 3 sliced onions

6 or 8 slices of diced bacon

4 apples, cored and cut into large chunks

A few cupfuls of applesauce (try the recipe on page 159)

A few cupfuls of chicken broth

A couple of chopped carrots

Half a bottle of white wine

A few heaping spoonfuls of any mustard (I prefer grainy)

2 or 3 bay leaves

A sprinkle or two of salt and pepper

SERVES SIX

Place a large Dutch oven or stew pot over medium-high heat. Splash in enough oil to coat the bottom with a thin layer. Blot the pork roast dry with paper towels so it will sear easily, then carefully add it to the hot oil. Brown it well on all sides. Be patient! This is the only opportunity you'll have to add the rich flavours of browned meat to the dish. When the roast is evenly browned, take it out of the pot and set it aside for a few minutes. Pour off as much of the fat in the pot as you can, then add the onions and bacon. Cook, stirring frequently, until the bacon and onions are nicely browned, about 15 minutes. If the bottom of the pot starts to brown too much, add a splash of water and turn the heat down a notch.

Return the pork roast to the pot. Add the apples, applesauce, chicken broth, carrots, wine, mustard and bay leaves. Season well with salt and pepper. Bring the works to a simmer, then place a tight-fitting lid on the pot and reduce the heat to the lowest setting that will maintain the simmer. Cook slowly until the meat is very tender, about 2 hours.

FEEL FREE TO TRY

Try adding a favourite herb or spice, such as cinnamon, nutmeg, rosemary or thyme to the pot. If you don't have any applesauce, just add a few more apples. If you don't have any chicken broth, try apple juice, cider or even water. If you need the burner space, you can place the pot in a 325°F (160°C) oven for several hours.

HINTS

The more an animal uses a particular muscle, the tougher it gets and thus the cheaper it is to buy. But the more a muscle is used the more flavour it develops! If necessary, sear one piece at a time so you don't overload your pot and impede browning.

GOES WELL WITH . . .
WHOLE WHEAT SPAETZLE page 112
BROWN RICE AND LENTILS page 115
ASPARAGUS RED ONION SALAD page 49

I THINK OF STEWED CHICKEN as a flavour sponge; on its own it's a bit bland, but braise it and it comes to life! Chicken will absorb just about any flavour but it really loves the earthy richness of mushrooms. This dish is a great way to get to know some of the other mushrooms that you see in the supermarket.

CHICKEN MUSHROOM STEW

A splash of olive oil

8 or 10 chicken thighs

A sprinkle or two of salt and pepper

2 chopped onions

A pound or so (500 g) of your favourite mushrooms, halved or quartered

A few chopped garlic cloves

A spoonful of minced fresh rosemary, sage or thyme

A cup or so of chicken broth

A cup or so of your favourite red or white wine

SERVES FOUR

Preheat a large skillet over a medium-high heat, then splash a thin layer of oil into it. Season the chicken thighs, then position them in the pan in a single layer—skin side down. Patiently brown them until each is golden brown on both sides, about 15 minutes in total. As each one finishes browning, remove it from the pan and set it aside until the rest finish.

Pour off most of the chicken fat, then add the onions and sauté them in the remaining fat until they turn golden brown, about 10 minutes. Add the mushrooms and garlic and continue to cook, stirring frequently. The mushrooms will release quite a bit of liquid; continue cooking until most of it evaporates away. This will dramatically concentrate the earthy flavours of the mushrooms.

Stir in the herbs, then return the chicken thighs to the pan along with the broth and wine. Adjust the heat to maintain a slow simmer; a fast boil will toughen the meat. Cover the pan with a tight-fitting lid so that no moisture escapes and cook until the meat is very tender and falling off the bone, about 45 minutes. Gently remove the bones from the chicken thighs and season the stew again before serving. Enjoy!

FEEL FREE TO TRY
Once the chicken is done stir in some thinly sliced green onions and a bit of chopped parsley for some last-minute green flavour. I also like to ladle it over a big handful of raw baby spinach leaves.

HINTS
This stew works with any mushroom, even the most common, regular white buttons. Whatever type you choose, don't slice them into oblivion–show off Mother Nature's form by halving or quartering them.

Sometimes as I brown chicken thighs the crisp skin falls off. If this happens to you, enjoy it as a treat for the cook and continue browning the exposed surface.

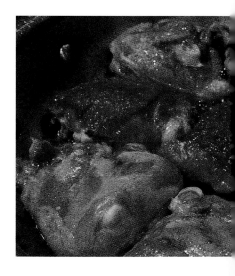

GOES WELL WITH . . .

WHOLE WHEAT SPAETZLE page 112

BROWN RICE AND LENTILS page 115

GARLIC-STEAMED BROCCOLI page 122

GOES WELL WITH . . .

ROASTED GARLIC BREAD page 133

ITALIAN BASIL SALAD page 43

CAESAR SALAD page 42

A GOOD FISH STEW has three basic parts: the flavour base, the broth and the fish. Each is easy to master. This one highlights many of the bright flavours of the Mediterranean. Some would call it a bouillabaisse but that makes it sound fancy and difficult. It's just a fish stew that tastes so good you'll forget what it's called anyway!

MEDITERRANEAN FISH STEW

To make the fish broth, cover the fish bones with 4 to 5 cups (1 to 1.25 L) of water and simmer for 20 minutes. Skim off and discard as much of the foam that rises to the surface as possible; it makes the broth murky. Strain and reserve the broth.

Splash some olive oil into a soup pot over a medium-high heat. Sauté the fennel, onions, garlic and fennel seeds until they soften and smell wonderful, about 5 minutes. Pour in the wine and simmer for another 5 minutes.

Add the tomatoes, hot pepper flakes, saffron, bay leaves, reserved fish stock and salt. Simmer for 20 minutes or so, just long enough for the flavours to brighten but not long enough for them to begin to dull.

At the last minute zest the orange into the stew and squeeze in the juice. Gently stir in the fish and simmer for another few minutes until it cooks through. Ladle away and enjoy!

FEEL FREE TO TRY

You can use any combination of your favourite fish or shellfish to make this stew. Salmon, white fish, scallops, shrimp and mussels are all wonderful. If you can't find fish bones it's okay to use water or even a light chicken broth.

HINTS

Fish bones release their flavours very quickly; they only need to simmer for 20 minutes, unlike meat bones, which need several hours. Unless it's tomato season in my backyard, I prefer the field-ripe flavour of canned tomatoes to their fresh but hard and bland cousins.

2 pounds or so (1 kg) of white fish bones from your local fishmonger

A splash of olive oil

A head of chopped fennel (discard the stringy stalks and woody core)

2 chopped onions

4 sliced garlic cloves

A few spoonfuls of fennel seeds

A cupful of any white wine

A 28-ounce (796-mL) can of chopped or puréed ripe tomatoes

A pinch of hot pepper flakes

Two pinches of saffron threads

2 or 3 bay leaves

A sprinkle or two of salt

The zest and juice of an orange

12 ounces (375 g) of halibut, cut into large chunks

12 ounces (375 g) of haddock, cut into large chunks

SERVES FOUR TO SIX

GOES WELL WITH . . .

FROZEN BUTTER BISCUITS page 134

ASPARAGUS RED ONION SALAD page 49

ASIAN SPINACH SALAD page 44

IN THE MARITIMES we don't worry whether our chowders are authentic or not. We know a true clam chowder is just a bowl full of simple, hearty flavours. We often use canned clams and always stir in onions, potatoes and milk. We're too busy asking for seconds to worry whether we got it right!

MARITIME CLAM CHOWDER

Toss the bacon into a heavy-bottomed soup pot with a splash of water. Stir on medium-high heat until it crisps nicely. Pour off most of the fat. Add another splash of water to loosen the flavourful bits on the bottom, then add the onion and celery. Sauté them for a few minutes until they soften and smell great.

Add the white wine, cream, milk and clams. Coarsely grate the potato with a standard box grater and add it along with the bay leaves and thyme. Bring the mixture to a slow simmer, stirring frequently. Turn the heat down a notch or two and continue simmering until the grated potato softens, releasing its starches and thickening the chowder, about 20 minutes.

Add the evaporated milk and continue stirring until it's heated through. Taste the chowder and season it well with salt and pepper. Stir in the parsley and serve immediately with your favourite biscuits.

FEEL FREE TO TRY

If you prefer a lower-fat version, you can replace the cream and the evaporated milk with regular milk. Try stirring in a handful of fresh dill with the parsley.

HINTS

Adding water to the raw bacon helps it gradually release its fat and brown evenly. This chowder can be made a day or two in advance and reheated. Its flavour actually gets better when it rests overnight. Baking potatoes are the best choice for thickening the chowder—their flesh is high in starch, low in moisture and dissolves easily.

4 slices of chopped bacon

A chopped onion

2 chopped celery stalks

A generous splash of any white wine

A cupful of heavy cream

A cupful of milk

Two 5-ounce (150-g) cans of clam meat

A large unpeeled baking potato

2 bay leaves

The leaves from 3 or 4 sprigs of fresh thyme

A 12-ounce (357-mL) can of unsweetened evaporated milk

A sprinkle or two of salt and pepper

A handful of flat-leaf parsley leaves

SERVES FOUR, WITH SECONDS

SALMON IS ONE OF THE HEALTHIEST foods you can cook for your family. We eat it every week and often crust it with cornmeal. Mussels travel with their own sauce. Steam them and they release a flavourful broth that's a quick and easy addition to any fish dish.

CORNMEAL-CRUSTED SALMON
WITH BASIL MUSSEL BROTH

2 to 3 pounds (1 to 1.5 kg) of fresh mussels

A big splash of any white wine

A big splash of cream

A sprinkle or two of salt and pepper

A few heaping spoonfuls of basil pesto (try the recipe on page 164)

A cup or so of fine cornmeal

Another sprinkle or two of salt and pepper

Four 6-ounce (175-g) skinless salmon fillets

A big splash of vegetable oil

SERVES FOUR·

Toss the mussels, wine and cream into a large pot over medium-high heat. Cover with a tight-fitting lid to capture the steam. Cook until the mussel shells pop open, about 5 minutes or so. Cool the mussels until you can handle them, then shuck away, tossing the shells and any lingering beards. Strain the broth into a saucepan. Bring the broth to a simmer, season it with salt and pepper and stir in the pesto and reserved mussel meat. Keep warm while you make the salmon.

Pour the cornmeal into a large resealable plastic bag with a pinch of salt and a generous sprinkle of pepper. Toss each salmon fillet one at a time with the cornmeal.

Preheat a large sauté pan over medium-high heat. Add enough cooking oil to cover the bottom of the pan. Carefully add the crusted fillets and pan-fry until crisp and golden on the first side, about 5 minutes. Turn the fillets and crisp the other side. Serve with a ladleful of the reheated mussel broth.

FEEL FREE TO TRY
Use any wine you like to flavour the mussel broth. The cream is optional—it adds richness—but the broth is still very flavourful without it. You can replace the basil pesto with a spoonful of any herb you fancy. Try adding a handful of fennel or poppy seeds to the cornmeal for a flavour twist.

HINTS
Most mussels are sold without their beards—those tough strands of thread they anchor themselves with. If yours are still attached, just tug them off. When you're crusting something, coarsely ground cornmeal doesn't adhere as well as finely ground cornmeal. When you're pan-frying the fish it's better to have a bit too much oil rather than too little. This will help the crust cook more evenly.

GOES WELL WITH . . .

CORN POLENTA page 119

WHOLE WHEAT SPAETZLE page 112

BASMATI RICE page 114

TUNA IS THE MOST LUXURIOUS FISH in the sea—fatty and smooth. I love it raw and to preserve its flavour I prefer not to cook it beyond medium rare. The sharp flavours of ginger and mint in the salsa contrast with the tuna's richness, adding a delicious bite to the dish.

PEPPERCORN-CRUSTED TUNA
WITH GINGER MINT SALSA

FOR THE SALSA

A ripe tomato

A small knob of grated fresh ginger

A bunch of chopped fresh mint

A thinly sliced green onion, including the white part

A splash of olive oil

The juice and zest of half a lemon

A sprinkle or two of salt

FOR THE TUNA

A spoonful of red pepper-corns

A spoonful of green pepper-corns

A spoonful of black pepper-corns

A spoonful of any coarse salt

Four 6-ounce (175-g) sushi-grade tuna steaks

A few splashes of vegetable oil

SERVES FOUR

Chop the tomato and toss with the remaining salsa ingredients. You'll be tempted to eat it right away, but save some to go with the tuna!

Process the peppercorns in an electric spice grinder or with a mortar and pestle. Crack them, but don't grind them into a powder. Mix the peppercorns and salt together and pour onto a plate. Press each tuna steak into the mixture, coating both sides well.

Meanwhile, preheat a large sauté pan over medium-high heat. Add a big splash of cooking oil and then the tuna steaks. Sear for no more than 3 minutes per side. Cook just long enough to form a crust but not long enough to allow the heat to penetrate and cook the centre of the fish. Serve with the salsa. Delicious!

FEEL FREE TO TRY

You can replace the peppercorns with whole fennel seeds; they make a wonderful crust. Try substituting fresh basil or oregano for the mint in the salsa.

HINTS

Ask your fishmonger to cut the tuna steaks as thick as possible. A thicker cut won't overcook in the time it takes to sear the outer crust of the fish. Use enough oil to thoroughly coat the pan—this will help form an even crust quickly.

GOES WELL WITH . . .

ASIAN SPINACH SALAD page 44

FENNEL SALAD page 46

BRAISED LEEKS page 127

GOES WELL WITH . . .

ROASTED GARLIC BREAD page 133

ITALIAN BASIL SALAD page 43

CAESAR SALAD page 42

YOU HAVEN'T LIVED until you've roasted a tomato! When you do you'll reveal a deep satisfying tomato flavour that will make this one of your favourite ways to dress pasta. My family loves the simple rustic flavours of this dish.

PENNE WITH ROAST TOMATOES

Preheat your oven to 400°F (200°C). Roll the meat up in a cigar shape, then thinly slice it. Toss it with the tomatoes, onions, garlic and olive oil. The meat will infuse the tomatoes with lots of flavour. Season the works with salt and pepper, then toss everything into a casserole dish.

Roast until the tomatoes shrivel and begin to brown a bit, about one hour. As they roast their flavours will concentrate and caramelize. The heat will also break them down a bit so they'll form a loose sauce when they're tossed with the pasta. When the tomatoes are done, discard any onion slices that may have blackened a bit—a small price to pay for the rich flavours of roasted tomato!

Cook the pasta in lots of boiling salted water. It's done when it's tender—but still a bit firm in the centre. Don't rinse it—that drains away valuable starch that helps the sauce adhere. Toss the hot pasta with the hot sauce and enjoy the tasty, roasted tomatoes!

4 or 5 slices of prosciutto, pancetta or ham

A dozen or so plum tomatoes, halved lengthwise

2 thinly sliced onions

4 minced garlic cloves

A generous splash of olive oil

A sprinkle or two of salt and pepper

One 16-ounce (500-g) box of penne pasta

SERVES FOUR

FEEL FREE TO TRY

For lots of bright flavour bursts, try tossing the tomatoes with a handful of fennel seeds before roasting them or toss the works with lots of whole basil leaves just before serving it.

HINTS

Make sure you cook your penne in a large pot with lots of boiling salted water. As the pasta cooks it will absorb the seasoned water and in turn be properly seasoned. A pinch or two of salt is not enough! Taste the water—it should remind you of a day at the beach!

GOES WELL WITH . . .
ROASTED GARLIC BREAD page 133
ITALIAN BASIL SALAD page 43
CAESAR SALAD page 42

EVERY COOK NEEDS A pasta meat sauce that tastes like it simmered all day long. This one's mine. But it has a speedy secret. The meat isn't browned! You can make it in less than an hour and everyone will still think you spent the day in the kitchen when they taste its rich, meaty flavour.

PASTA WITH SPEEDY MEAT SAUCE

Cut the pancetta, bacon or prosciutto Into small pieces, then toss them into a saucepot with a splash of oil. Cook over medium heat, stirring frequently, until crisp and golden brown. This will infuse the sauce with a touch of browned meat flavour.

Process the onions, carrots, celery, garlic and mushrooms with another splash of olive oil in your food processor until they're finely chopped and almost puréed. Toss into the pot and sauté for a few minutes until they smell great. Add the meat, wine, bay leaves, oregano, salt and pepper. Stir vigorously, breaking the meat up into small pieces. Bring to a simmer and continue cooking until the liquid reduces by at least half.

Add the canned tomatoes along with the tomato paste to the sauce. Season with a touch of salt and pepper. Simmer until the sauce thickens and the flavours blend together, about 30 minutes. Taste the sauce and add a touch more salt and pepper if necessary. Serve with your favourite pasta.

FEEL FREE TO TRY

You can add a few large pinches of dried oregano to the sauce as it simmers. Don't use dried basil though; it has very little flavour. If you don't have a food processor, chop the vegetables as finely as you can by hand.

HINTS

Because the meat never browns it doesn't toughen and require hours of simmering to tenderize—but it still adds body and richness. Pasta absorbs moisture as it cooks, so don't forget to use lots of heavily salted boiling water. Don't rinse the pasta—that drains away valuable starch that helps the sauce adhere.

A few slices of pancetta, bacon or prosciutto

A few splashes of olive oil

A few onions, cut into large chunks

A couple of carrots, cut into large chunks

A couple of stalks of celery, cut into large chunks

3 or 4 garlic cloves

A few handfuls of button mushrooms

1 ½ pounds (750 g) of ground meat, either pork, veal, or beef or any combination of the three

A cup or so of your favourite red wine

2 or 3 bay leaves

A heaping spoonful of dried oregano

A sprinkle or two of salt and pepper

A 28-ounce (796-mL) can of puréed tomatoes

A small can of tomato paste

SERVES SIX WITH LEFTOVERS

THAI COOKS LIKE easy-to-make dishes just as much as Western cooks do. That's why I love this dish. It's packed full of easy flavours. Once you get to know the ingredients you'll appreciate its simplicity as much as I do! Lime leaves, lemon grass, fish sauce and curry paste add lots of authentic flavour and are both easily found in Asian markets.

94

THAI CURRY NOODLE BOWL

Two 14-ounce (398-mL) cans of premium coconut milk

A heaping spoonful of red, green or yellow Thai curry paste

1 bunch of cilantro, roots and leaves chopped separately

2 thinly sliced chicken breasts

A few cupfuls of chicken broth

A shredded carrot

4 or 5 lime leaves

2 lemon grass stalks (cut in half lengthwise and peel off any woody outer leaves)

A few spoonfuls of fish sauce

The juice and zest of 2 limes

A small knob of frozen ginger

A handful of bean sprouts

An 8-ounce (250-g) package of rice noodles

A sprinkle or two of salt or soy sauce

2 or 3 thinly sliced green onions

SERVES FOUR

Scoop the thick coconut cream from the top of one of the cans into a large saucepan or wok set over medium-high heat. Melt the cream, add the curry paste and stir for a few minutes until they begin to sizzle. Add the cilantro roots and chicken. Sauté until the chicken is cooked through, about 5 minutes.

Add the coconut milk from the first can and all the contents of the second can with the chicken broth, carrot, lime leaves, lemon grass, fish sauce and lime. Grate the frozen ginger into the broth with a microplane grater or standard box grater. Simmer for 20 minutes or so.

Stir in the bean sprouts. Add the rice noodles, gently pushing them beneath the surface of the broth. Turn off the heat and let stand until the noodles soften, about 5 minutes. Stir in most of the cilantro leaves, reserving a few for garnish. Remove the lemon grass stalks. Taste and season with a touch more salt or soy sauce as needed. Ladle into large bowls and garnish with the green onions and remaining cilantro.

FEEL FREE TO TRY

Try stirring in a head of chopped bok choy or a bag of baby spinach with the bean sprouts. If you don't have a knob of frozen ginger or a microplane grater, it's okay to simply grate a fresh knob on a standard box grater.

HINTS

Stirring the curry paste into the hot coconut oil brightens the curry's flavours and slightly reduces its heat level. Red curry paste is slightly milder than green curry paste. Rice noodles don't need to simmer like pasta to cook, they simply need to rehydrate in hot liquid.

GOES WELL WITH . . .

GOES WELL WITH . . .

ASPARAGUS RED ONION SALAD page 49

FROZEN BUTTER BISCUITS page 134

FENNEL SALAD page 46

MY FAMILY ENJOYS the rich, healthy flavours of vegetarian-style meals several times a week. This soup is one of our favourites. It features complementary grains and legumes so it provides a complete protein profile. Translation? Healthy, vegetarian food tastes great and is easy to make.

VEGETARIAN PROTEIN SOUP

To make the broth, add the olive oil to a large soup pot over medium-high heat. Add the celery, onions, carrots, fennel and mushrooms and sauté until they start to colour a bit, about 15 minutes. The high heat will brighten and deepen their flavours. Add the garlic and sauté for another few minutes. (Because garlic burns so quickly it's always best to add it last.) Add the wine, herbs and enough water to submerge the vegetables by several inches, about 8 cups (2 L) or so. Season with salt and pepper. Simmer until the broth is infused with the flavours of the vegetables, about 30 minutes. Strain and use immediately, refrigerate or freeze.

For the soup, sauté the carrots, celery and onions with a bit of olive oil in a soup pot over medium-high heat. Cover until they soften, about 5 minutes. Add the broth, rice and lentils. Bring the works to a simmer and continue cooking until the rice and lentils are tender, about 30 minutes. Just before serving, stir in the corn, peas and parsley. Cook just long enough to heat them through; that way they'll keep their bright colour and fresh flavours. Taste the soup and season as needed with a touch more salt and pepper.

FOR THE BROTH

A splash of olive oil

A few stalks of thinly sliced celery

A few thinly sliced onions

A few diced carrots

A thinly sliced head of fennel, fronds removed, core sliced out

A handful of sliced button mushrooms

3 or 4 sliced garlic cloves

A cup or so of white wine

A few sprigs of fresh thyme

A few bay leaves

A sprinkle or two of salt and pepper

FOR THE SOUP

A couple of diced carrots

A couple of diced celery stalks

A couple of sliced onions

A splash of olive oil

Half a cup or so of brown rice

Half a cup or so of lentils

A cupful of fresh or frozen corn

A cupful of fresh or frozen peas

1 bunch of flat-leaf parsley

A sprinkle or two of salt and pepper

MAKES SOUP FOR FOUR

FEEL FREE TO TRY

For a lighter-bodied soup you can replace the vegetable broth with water. If you want a fuller-bodied version, use chicken broth, but of course it won't be vegetarian anymore. Toss in a handful of your favourite herbs for a flavour boost. Try stirring a bag of baby spinach or other savoury green into the soup with the peas and corn.

HINTS

Meat contains the basic building blocks of protein, but a complete vegetarian protein profile can be achieved by mixing grains such as rice and corn with legumes like lentils, peas or beans.

HOMEMADE PIZZA IS SIMPLE to make and a lot more fun than just picking up the phone. Impress your family and turn your kitchen into a pizza parlour with a ball of store-bought dough and this easy-to-make sauce. If you're as serious about pizza as I am, you'll get the best results with a pizza stone and a pizza paddle.

PIZZA PARLOUR PIZZA

One 16-ounce (500-g) ball of frozen pizza dough

A finely diced onion

A generous splash of olive oil

3 or 4 minced garlic cloves

A small can of tomato paste

A small can of crushed ripe tomatoes

A heaping spoonful of dried oregano

A sprinkle or two of salt and pepper

Toppings of your choice

A few cups of grated mozzarella cheese

MAKES ENOUGH FOR TWO MEDIUM THIN-CRUST PIZZAS, OR ONE LARGE THICK-CRUST PIZZA WITH LEFTOVER SAUCE

Take the dough out of the freezer a day or 2 or the night before you need it. Refrigerate it in the bag until it thaws and begins to swell. Meanwhile, sauté the onions with the oil in a saucepot over medium-high heat. When they soften and begin to turn golden, add the garlic and stir for a further minute or two. Add the tomato paste, tomatoes and oregano and bring the sauce to a simmer. Season with salt and pepper, then continue simmering until the flavours blend together, another 15 minutes or so.

Meanwhile, preheat your oven and pizza stone to 400°F (200°C) and form the dough into a pizza round. I find it easiest to focus on pinching a thin outer edge while allowing the middle to take care of itself with all the stretching. You can also dust a work surface with lots of flour and roll the dough out with a rolling pin. You won't end up with a perfect round pie but that's okay. Hand-made looks better! If you like, divide the dough into two pieces and make a smaller thin-crust pizza out of each. When you're done, sprinkle your pizza paddle with cornmeal and stretch the dough out on it. The cornmeal will help keep the dough from sticking.

Spread a few heaping spoonfuls of sauce evenly across the dough. Not too much though—you don't want a soggy pizza! Add your favourite toppings and an even sprinkling of grated mozzarella cheese. Place the paddle on the pre-heated stone and with one hand begin pushing the pizza off. With the other hand quickly and steadily pull away the paddle, dropping the pizza onto the stone. At first the dough will stick to the stone but it will release as it bakes. Bake until the pizza begins to brown and it can be easily moved around the stone, about 20 minutes.

FEEL FREE TO TRY

The sky's the limit for toppings! Meats, vegetables and different cheeses are all fair game. Try not to weigh the pizza down with too many toppings and too much cheese though. A little bit goes a long way.

HINTS

Oregano is the only herb that tastes better dried; I prefer its sharper flavour to the milder taste of fresh oregano. Pizza stones absorb the oven's heat and slowly radiate it back, helping to form a beautiful crust. The paddle makes it very easy to move the pizza around. If you don't have a stone and a paddle, simply place the dough on a large baking sheet, add the toppings and bake until it's done. It works, but the bottom crisps better with a stone. I find that if you let the frozen dough thaw and rest for a fews days in the refrigerator, it's much easier to work with.

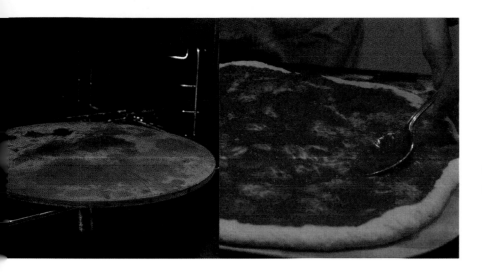

GOES WELL WITH . . .
CAESAR SALAD page 42
ITALIAN BASIL SALAD page 43
BROWNIES page 146

GOES WELL WITH . . .

GARLIC-STEAMED BROCCOLI page 122

ZUCCHINI WITH TOMATOES AND OREGANO page 121

CAESAR SALAD page 42

FEW THINGS ARE AS GOOD as a steaming bowl of homemade macaroni and cheese, especially when it doesn't come out of a box! I don't normally put lobster in mine—and this version is great without my favourite crustacean—but it's a delicious way to make the ordinary extraordinary!

MAC AND CHEESE WITH LOBSTER

Preheat your oven to 350°F (180°C). Meanwhile, cook the pasta in lots of boiling, well-salted water. Cook the pasta until it's tender but still a bit firm in the centre; it will finish cooking in the sauce. Drain it well but don't rinse.

Melt the butter in a saucepan over medium heat, add the garlic and stir for several minutes as it softens and flavours the butter. Add the flour and stir with a wooden spoon until a smooth paste forms (the roux). Continue cooking a few more minutes as the roux toasts and develops a bit of flavour. Slowly stir in the wine and continue mixing until the mixture is smooth again. Add both milks and switch to a whisk, mixing until smooth yet again. Continue whisking until the mixture is very thick, a few minutes longer. Stir in the paprika, Dijon, cayenne, cheese and salt.

Stir the lobster meat into the cheese mixture along with the pasta. Pour everything into a 9 by 13-inch (3.5-L) ovenproof baking dish. Toss the bread with a bit of olive oil, then sprinkle it evenly over the top of the mixture. Bake until the casserole is heated through and the breadcrumbs are golden brown, about 30 minutes.

A 1-pound (500-g) box of penne pasta

A stick of butter (4 ounces/125 g)

2 chopped garlic cloves

$\frac{2}{3}$ cup (150 mL) of flour

A big splash of any white wine

A 12-ounce (357-mL) can of evaporated milk

4 cups (1 L) of milk

A heaping spoonful of paprika

A few heaping spoonfuls of Dijon mustard

A pinch of cayenne pepper

1 pound (500 g) or so of grated aged cheddar cheese

A sprinkle or two of salt

2 or 3 lobsters, steamed, shelled and chopped

Half a loaf of Italian bread, hand-torn into small pieces

A generous splash of olive oil

SERVES FOUR TO SIX

FEEL FREE TO TRY

Try substituting other semi-firm cheeses, like Swiss, Jack or Emmental, for the cheddar. Just about any minced fresh herb will add a wonderful aroma to the cheese sauce; I like thyme, tarragon and dill. You can replace the lobster with lots of thinly sliced ham or a can or two of clams or a bag of shrimp. If you use clams, replace some of the milk with their juice.

HINTS

Combining the flour and butter into a roux helps evenly distribute the flour throughout the sauce, preventing lumps. Aged cheddar cheese adds much more flavour than blander mild cheddar.

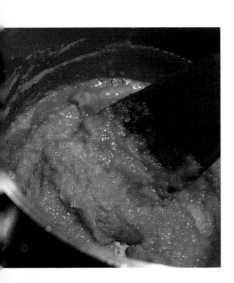

SIDES

EVERY GREAT DINNER DISH needs a good sidekick—a vegetable dish or two to back up the star of the meal. On a good night, a creative side dish can even steal the show!

We bring vegetables to my family's table every day. We treasure their awesome goodness. Their colourful, feel-good flavours will look great on your table too.

The next time you're in the grocery store, experiment and take home a vegetable you've never tried before! They'll get along great with the other interesting flavours in your refrigerator.

These are some of my favourite dishes. They're full of simple, familiar flavours. I often make them without a recipe, and you can too! Try pairing them with other delicious recipes in this book.

THIS DISH WAS CREATED as a way to use up leftover boiled or baked potatoes, but it's so good that now I cook potatoes just so I can smash and crisp them. If you like crispy potatoes, you'll love this simple method.

SMASHED POTATOES

A baked or boiled skin-on potato

A spoonful of olive, corn or canola oil

A sprinkle or two of salt and pepper

SERVES ONE PERSON

If you don't have any leftover potatoes, simply bake a few until tender in a 400°F (200°C) oven. Alternatively, steam or microwave them.

Preheat your oven to 450°F (230°C). Place the cooked potatoes on a lightly oiled baking sheet. Push down on each one with a small flat plate until the potato smashes and spreads out to about twice its original size. You can also use a potato masher if you have one. If a few pieces get loose, just push them back into the potato.

Drizzle each potato with lots of oil and season with salt and pepper. Bake until the exposed potato flesh crisps and turns golden brown, about 30 to 40 minutes.

FEEL FREE TO TRY
Try sprinkling whole fennel seeds over the potatoes. You'll love their soft chewy texture and delicate licorice-like flavour.

HINTS
You can use a freshly cooked potato, but it's best if you cool it first. A cool potato doesn't crumble as much when it's smashed—it tends to stay together in one big piece.

THIS IS A TASTY SIDE DISH that can be banged out in five minutes. Couscous is a tiny type of cracked, granular pasta that's already been cooked and dried. It's actually easier to use than other pastas. Just soak it in some boiling liquid and it's good to go!

COUSCOUS

Pour the water and tomatoes into a small pot and bring them to a boil. Turn off the heat, then stir in the couscous. Cover it and let it rest for 10 minutes while its tiny grains absorb moisture.

When the couscous has rehydrated and tenderized, stir in the parsley, lemon, olive oil and seasoning. If there are any leftovers, put them in the refrigerator; they'll be even tastier tomorrow!

A cupful of lightly salted boiling water

A cupful of chopped dried tomatoes

A cupful of couscous

A handful of chopped flat-leaf parsley

The juice and zest from half a lemon

A splash of extra virgin olive oil

A sprinkle or two of salt and pepper

MAKES ENOUGH FOR FOUR SIDES OR TWO MAINS

FEEL FREE TO TRY

Couscous is a neutral base that's at its best when carrying other bright flavours. Try any fresh herb you can find. I like basil, oregano and even mint. Stir in minced kalamata olives, capers or a tasty minced pickle! For richer flavour, use simmering chicken broth instead of water.

HINTS

Make sure the water is pleasantly seasoned. The couscous will absorb it and in turn be seasoned perfectly. A fork works best when stirring the couscous. It helps break up any clumps and fluff it up.

EVERYBODY KNOWS HOW GOOD mashed potatoes are but if you really want to impress your friends and family, try them with brown butter. You won't believe how much flavour is locked into a stick of butter but you will believe these are the best mashed spuds you've ever had!

BROWN BUTTER MASHED POTATOES

2 pounds (1 kg) or so of unpeeled potatoes (about 4 large)

A stick or 2 of salted butter (4 ounces/125 g)

A few pinches of nutmeg

A sprinkle or two of salt and pepper

SERVES FOUR

Cut the potatoes into large chunks, then steam, boil or microwave them until they're tender. Drain well.

Meanwhile, toss the butter into a small saucepot and heat it until it melts over medium heat. Because butter contains as much as 20 percent water it will begin to steam and foam. Once the water has evaporated, the foam will subside and the butter's temperature will begin to rise. The milk fat solids, which are 1 or 2 percent of the butter, will then begin to brown. Continue watching as it begins foaming a second time. Swirl it gently, watching the colour, until it turns golden brown and releases the aroma of toasting nuts. Immediately pour the browned butter into a bowl to stop it from browning further.

When the potatoes are tender, mash in the butter, nutmeg and seasonings. Taste and season a bit more if needed. Then watch the bowl empty!

FEEL FREE TO TRY
You can peel the potatoes if you prefer but you'll lose some rustic flavour and some nutrients if you do. Your choice! Sliced green onions and chopped parsley add both flavour and colour. French chefs always add a pinch of elegant nutmeg to their potato purées.

HINTS
The best potatoes for mashing are the low-moisture, high-starch varieties that are also the best for baking. My favourite is Yukon Gold. Its creamy texture and golden colour are perfect with the brown butter.

THIS SPECIAL-OCCASION TREAT features the classic trio of potatoes, bacon and cheddar. It does take a while to make but the results are worth it. It may look difficult, but you'll soon realize how simple it is to master!

POTATO BACON CHEDDAR TART

Preheat your oven to 350°F (180°C). Carefully arrange the bacon in a radial pattern from the centre of a 10-inch (25-cm), non-stick tart pan to the rim. Continue up and over the rim letting the ends hang over. The slices should overlap slightly around the sides of the pan. To reduce the thickness of the bacon in the centre, stagger every other piece, starting it 2 inches (5 cm) from the centre and extending it further than the adjacent slice. With the palm of your hand, flatten the centre area, leaving no gaps in the bacon. Season the bacon with pepper, then sprinkle on several tablespoons of the grated cheddar.

Slice the potatoes as thinly and uniformly as you can, about ¼ inch (5 mm) thick. Arrange a circular pattern of overlapping slices around the bottom edge of the pan. Continue arranging overlapping layers of the potatoes until the bottom is evenly covered. Season the potatoes with salt and pepper. Mix the onion and garlic together and sprinkle some of the mixture onto the potatoes. Continue with a layer of the grated cheese. Cover with another layer of potato, pressing it down firmly. Continue alternating layers of potatoes, onion mixture and cheese insetting each a bit from the edge of the pan, until the pan is full and the top is an inch or so higher than the pan's rim. Fold the overhanging bacon neatly up and over the top of the potatoes. Trim a small piece of parchment paper and place it between an ovenproof lid and the bacon. This will prevent the bacon from pulling back and shrinking during cooking.

Place the tart pan on a baking sheet and bake for at least 2 ½ to 3 hours. You'll know it's done when you can easily insert a small, thin-bladed knife. Pour off as much of the fat around the edges as possible. Let the tart stand for 15 minutes, then invert it onto a cutting surface. Slice into wedges and serve immediately. Refrigerate any leftovers and reheat them later in a microwave.

2 pounds (1 kg) or so of room temperature bacon

A sprinkle or two of pepper

4 cups or so of grated aged cheddar

5 or 6 large unpeeled baking potatoes

A sprinkle of salt and pepper to taste

A minced onion

3 minced garlic cloves

SERVES EIGHT

FEEL FREE TO TRY

Try mixing a few tablespoons of your favourite herb into the onion mixture. Thyme, rosemary and tarragon all work well.

HINTS

Kitchen specialty stores carry a fancy French chef's tool known as a mandoline. It easily slices the potatoes into even rounds. It's not necessary, though; a sharp knife works well too!

A GRILLED VEGETABLE SKEWER is one of the best ways I know to get kids to eat vegetables—especially when they're marinated in a tasty herb vinaigrette. Just about any veggie will grill nicely, so use your imagination and get ready for empty plates.

GRILLED VEGETABLE SKEWERS

If you're using wooden skewers, presoak them in water for an hour or so; this will help keep them from burning on the grill.

Cut the vegetables into roughly equal-sized chunks, then arrange as you wish on the skewers. Brush with the vinaigrette and let them marinate for an hour or so. Season with salt and pepper, then grill until the vegetables are lightly caramelized and tender.

FEEL FREE TO TRY
Broccoli and cauliflower are tasty but need to be precooked a bit before skewering; they take much longer to cook than squash or peppers.

HINTS
If the grill flames up a bit while you're grilling the skewers, simply sprinkle water on the flames until they subside. If you don't have a grill, arrange the skewers in a single layer on a baking sheet and roast in a preheated 450°F (230°C) oven until they're caramelized, about 30 minutes.

1 or 2 bell peppers

A zucchini or yellow squash

A red onion

A handful of cherry tomatoes

A handful of mushrooms

A few generous splashes of Red Wine Herb Vinaigrette (page 54)

A generous sprinkle of salt and pepper

MAKES EIGHT SKEWERS

SPAETZLE IS A TYPE OF GERMAN DUMPLING and a cousin of pasta. It's very easy to make and a great way to soak up the juices of any stew or braised dish. You can make it with plain flour, but I prefer whole wheat. It's tastier and better for you.

WHOLE WHEAT SPAETZLE

2 cups (500 mL) of whole wheat flour

1 cup (250 mL) of all-purpose flour

1 tablespoon of baking powder

A spoonful of ground nutmeg

A sprinkle or two of salt and pepper

4 large eggs

A cupful of milk

SERVES FOUR TO SIX

Bring a large pot of salted water to a boil. While you're waiting for it to boil whisk the dry ingredients together until they're thoroughly combined. In a separate bowl whisk the eggs and milk together. Add the egg mixture to the dry ingredients and stir with the end of a wooden spoon until the batter is completely mixed and seems a bit elastic.

Using a rubber spatula, force some of the batter through the holes of a colander or box grater into the boiling water. The batter will form irregular strands, sink and almost immediately rise to the surface. That's how you know they're done. Take them out with a strainer or slotted spoon. Continue until all the batter is used.

Spoon into a bowl and top with a ladleful of stew, a touch of melted butter or a splash of olive oil. Try to leave some leftovers!

FEEL FREE TO TRY
For slightly lighter results, you can use water instead of milk and all-purpose flour instead of whole wheat. You can also toast the spaetzle by sautéing it in a non-stick pan for a few minutes with melted butter or olive oil.

HINTS
Whisking the dry ingredients together first ensures even distribution of the salt and baking powder. Don't worry if some of the dumplings float a bit longer than others; they can handle it! The end of the wooden spoon mixes the dough without overmixing, which is what happens when using the bowl of the spoon.

THERE ARE MANY TYPES OF RICE but my family's favourite is basmati. The delicious, nutty aroma inspired its name, which in Sanskrit means "queen of fragrance." It's as easy to cook as it is to find, and if it isn't already, it soon will be one of your family's favourites.

114

BASMATI RICE

1 cup (250 mL) of white basmati rice

2 cups (500 mL) of water

A sprinkle or two of salt and pepper

MAKES ENOUGH FOR FOUR

Toss the rice into a small pot. Add the water and a touch of seasoning. Bring to a simmer, cover with a tight-fitting lid and cook until tender over very low heat, about 20 minutes.

Turn off the heat and let rest for 5 more minutes.

FEEL FREE TO TRY
For added richness add a spoonful of miso paste to the rice before simmering it or use chicken broth instead of water. For an exotic lime aroma add a few lime leaves before simmering. Sprinkle sliced almonds on top before serving.

HINTS
As the rice cooks, don't stir it; rubbing the grains together makes them sticky. There are many types of rice. This method works with just about any variety of white rice including the aromatic, easily found jasmine.

BROWN RICE STILL HAS its nutrient-rich bran and germ attached, so it has more flavour, colour and nutrients than polished white rice. Not only is it much tastier—with a deep nutty flavour—it's dramatically healthier. My family loves it!

BROWN RICE

1 cup (250 mL) of brown rice

A sprinkle or two of salt

2 ½ cups (675 mL) of water

MAKES FOUR SERVINGS

Toss the rice into a small pot; add a pinch of salt and the water. Bring to a boil over medium heat, then reduce the heat to the lowest setting that sustains a simmer. Cover with a tight-fitting lid and cook until tender, about 40 minutes.

Turn off the heat and let the rice rest, covered, for a few minutes before serving it. We drench ours with olive oil!

FEEL FREE TO TRY
For richer flavour, replace the water with chicken broth. For some exotic fun, add a pinch of cinnamon, a handful of raisins and a spoonful of orange marmalade to the rice before simmering it.

HINTS
Don't lift the lid to peek. It lets out all the steam, which means it will take longer to cook.

RICE IS A GRAIN, lentils are legumes. Combine the two and you have a perfect source of vegetarian protein. Of course, you don't have to be a vegetarian to enjoy the wholesome, tasty richness of this healthy duo.

BROWN RICE AND LENTILS

Pour the brown rice into a small pot with the water and a pinch of salt and pepper. Slowly simmer over medium-low heat for **15 minutes**.

Add the lentils and continue cooking until both the rice and lentils are tender and fluffy, another **30 minutes**.

½ cup (125 mL) of brown rice

2 cups (500 mL) of water

A sprinkle or two of salt and pepper

½ cup (125 mL) of green lentils

MAKES FOUR SERVINGS

FEEL FREE TO TRY

For even more vegetarian protein, stir frozen peas–another legume–and frozen corn–a grain–into the rice and lentils when they're almost done simmering. For richness and body, use chicken stock instead of water. Try adding any aromatic herb that strikes your fancy. Bay leaf, thyme and rosemary are some of my favourites.

HINTS

If at the end of the cooking time the mixture is a bit moist, turn the heat to high for a few minutes and stir until it dries out.

BARLEY IS AN ANCIENT grain with an addictive nutty taste and a pleasing chewy texture. This dish isn't a true risotto—because it doesn't include rice—but it's made the same way so I call it one. This is a great way to enjoy tasty and healthy whole grains.

BARLEY ASPARAGUS RISOTTO

4 slices of finely sliced bacon

A finely chopped onion

2 minced garlic cloves

1 cup (250 mL) of pearl barley

½ cup (125 mL) of your favourite white wine

6 cups (1.5 L) of chicken stock or water

A spoonful of minced fresh thyme

A bunch of asparagus, cut into 1-inch (2.5-cm) slices

A sprinkle or two of salt and pepper

½ cup (125 mL) of a top-notch grated Parmesan cheese like Grana Padano

MAKES FOUR SERVINGS

Add the bacon with a splash of water to a medium saucepan. Cook over medium heat, stirring frequently, until the bacon is crisp and lightly browned. If the pan begins to burn, add another splash of water and continue cooking. When the bacon is crisp, add the onion and garlic and continue cooking until they soften, about 5 minutes. Reduce the heat to medium-low, then add the barley and stir for a minute. Add the wine and stir until the liquid is absorbed.

In a separate pan warm the stock or water. Add 2 cupfuls of the liquid to the barley and slowly simmer, stirring frequently, until it's absorbed. Repeat with the remaining liquid, half a cupful at a time, simmering and stirring until each addition is absorbed before adding the next. If you run out of stock and the barley is still a bit crunchy, add hot water until it's tender or heat some more stock. The risotto may be made to this point in advance, then refrigerated.

Just before serving stir in the thyme, asparagus and seasoning. Cover with a lid, then continue cooking just long enough to heat the asparagus through, turning it bright green and tender. Stir in the cheese and serve immediately.

FEEL FREE TO TRY

If you'd like to make a vegetarian version, replace the bacon with a splash of olive oil and use water instead of chicken broth.

HINTS

The constant stirring and addition of liquid encourages the barley to release creamy starches that thicken the risotto and give it its characteristic smooth texture.

POLENTA IS A TRADITIONAL Italian pudding thickened with cornmeal. Freshly made, it has a soft creamy texture, but it hardens when cool and is then easily cut into slices that can be grilled or pan-seared. This method cuts the traditional hour-long stirring time in half by finishing the polenta in an oven.

CORN POLENTA

Preheat your oven to 350°F (180°C). Heat the oil in a large saucepan over medium heat. Add the onion and cook, stirring, until it just begins to turn golden brown, about 5 minutes. Add the milk and broth and bring them to a simmer.

Add the cornmeal in a slow steady stream, whisking constantly to prevent lumping. Switch to a wooden spoon as soon as all the cornmeal is in the broth. It will quickly thicken beyond the point that a whisk is useful. Lower the heat and continue cooking, stirring constantly, until the mixture really thickens, about 10 minutes.

Stir in the corn, cheese, salt and pepper, then pour into a loaf pan or baking dish. Bake for 15 minutes, rest for 5 minutes and serve while hot and creamy. Alternatively, refrigerate until firm, cut into slices and reheat on the grill. You can also toss the slices with more cornmeal and pan-fry them.

A splash of vegetable oil

A chopped onion

2 cups (500 mL) of milk

2 cups (500 mL) of chicken broth

A cupful of coarse yellow cornmeal

A cupful of frozen corn

Half a cupful of top-notch Parmesan cheese such as Grana Padano

A sprinkle or two of salt and pepper

SERVES FOUR TO SIX WITH LEFT-OVERS

FEEL FREE TO TRY

For a lighter polenta, you can substitute water for some or all of the milk or chicken broth. For more flavour, stir in a cupful of aged cheddar cheese and some crisp bacon bits. You can also stir in a few spoonfuls of pesto or lots of your favourite herb, chopped.

HINTS

Smooth polenta takes patience as you wait for the corn granules to swell and soften. In this recipe there are four parts liquid for every part cornmeal. The liquid will thicken faster if you add more cornmeal—a three to one ratio—but the finished texture will be a bit coarse.

FOR A TASTY SUMMER GARDEN treat any time of the year, nothing beats this quick sauté of zucchini and tomatoes. The key to its flavour is the high-heat caramelization of the zucchini and ripe tomatoes.

ZUCCHINI WITH TOMATOES AND OREGANO

Preheat a large thick sauté pan over high heat for a few minutes. Cut the zucchini in half lengthwise, then cut it into 2-inch (5-cm) long chunks. Add enough oil to the pan to coat the bottom, then immediately add the zucchini pieces face down. Cook for a few minutes. This will give the zucchini a chance to caramelize and develop a beautiful roasted flavour.

When you're pleased with the zucchini, add the tomatoes and onion. If you're using dried oregano, add it now as well. Lower the heat a notch or two, cover with a tight-fitting lid and continue cooking until the onion softens, about 5 minutes. Season with salt and pepper and if you choose, fresh oregano.

2 large green zucchinis

A large splash of olive oil

2 or 3 tomatoes cut into quarters

A sliced onion

A spoonful of minced fresh or dried oregano

A sprinkle or two of salt and pepper

SERVES FOUR WITH LEFTOVERS

FEEL FREE TO TRY

Thinly sliced fresh basil leaves added at the last second are a tasty substitute for the oregano. In the middle of winter, I prefer the flavour of canned tomatoes.

HINTS

Dried oregano needs a few minutes with the onions and tomatoes so its flavours can bloom.

If you add the zucchini to a cold pan it will gradually heat up with the pan and never achieve the high temperature needed for browning. A thicker pan will absorb more heat than a thin one and brown the zucchini better.

THIS IS MY FAVOURITE WAY to enjoy broccoli. As it quickly steams, it's scented with garlic—but not overwhelmed by it. It's also a quick way to turn a head of broccoli into a side dish. You can have it on the table in under 10 minutes!

122

GARLIC-STEAMED BROCCOLI

1 head of broccoli

A splash of olive oil

A clove or two of thinly sliced garlic

A sprinkle or two of salt and pepper

SERVES FOUR

Cut the broccoli into florets, discarding the tough stems. Splash enough water into a small saucepan to barely cover the bottom. Add the oil, garlic, salt and pepper, then begin heating over medium high heat. In a few moments—when the water starts to simmer—add the broccoli and cover the pot with a tight-fitting lid.

Steam until the broccoli is tender and bright green, about 5 minutes. The water should finish evaporating just as the broccoli finishes cooking. Remove the pan from the heat and give it a good shake. Serve immediately.

FEEL FREE TO TRY
For an exotic flavour burst, splash in a bit of strongly flavoured sesame oil instead of the olive oil.

HINTS
Simmering the garlic in water for a few moments helps it lose its pungency while releasing its aroma.

IN MY HOUSE, any time steak is on the menu, so are these mushrooms. They have all the flavours I love with beef—meaty mushrooms, browned onions and aromatic sherry. Your home will smell like a mouth-watering steakhouse!

MUSHROOMS, ONIONS AND SHERRY

Toss the butter and onions into a large sauté pan. Add a splash of water, place over medium-high heat and cover with a tight-fitting lid. In a few minutes the water will turn to steam, encouraging the onions to release their moisture. Take a peek. When the contents look like onion soup, remove the lid and allow the liquid to evaporate, stirring frequently. In a few minutes the moisture will disappear and the sugar in the onions will begin to brown. Toss the pan frequently and turn the heat down a notch as the browning starts. The onions will take about half an hour in total, so be patient!

Meanwhile, trim the mushrooms and cut them in half. When the onions are golden brown, add the mushrooms and sherry to the pan. Toss and cover with the lid again. After a few minutes the mushrooms will release lots of moisture. Remove the lid and continue cooking until the sherry liquid evaporates and forms a sauce.

Season with salt and pepper and serve immediately.

A few spoonfuls of butter

2 large sliced onions

A few large handfuls of assorted mushrooms

A big splash or two of sherry

A sprinkle or two of salt and pepper

SERVES FOUR

FEEL FREE TO TRY
Use any mushrooms you like but don't chop them and lose the form Mother Nature gave them—cut them in halves or quarters. If you use shiitakes, be sure to remove the woody stems. Whatever type you choose, feel free to wash them in lots of cold water. They're already mostly water, so they won't absorb any more!

HINTS
Patience is the key to browning onions. At first they're very pungent but they soon become quite bland and only when they begin browning do they regain any flavour. Gradually turn the heat down as they brown and they won't burn.

LEEKS ARE ONE OF THOSE vegetables you see at the store but you're not really sure what to do with them. After you taste their rich, buttery tenderness, you'll put them in your cart every time you go shopping!

BRAISED LEEKS

Preheat a large sauté pan over medium-high heat for a few minutes. Meanwhile, prepare the leeks. Trim off the roots, leaving the bottom intact. Cut off the leafy tops just past the point where they turn from white to light green—but before they turn dark green. Cut in half lengthwise. Rinse under cold running water, removing any dirt, mud or sand nestled in the layers. Blot dry.

Add enough oil to cover the pan. Place the leeks cut side down in a single layer. If they don't fit nicely, it's better to do a second batch than to crowd the pan. Sear until they're golden brown, then flip them over and sear the other side. When they're all beautifully coloured, discard as much oil as possible. Add the red wine, season and cover with a tight-fitting lid. Lower the heat and simmer them until they're tender. In 20 minutes or so you'll be able to easily poke a knife in them.

Gently remove the leeks from the pan, then turn up the heat. Add the cream, swirling until a sauce forms and thickens. Pour over the leeks and serve immediately.

4 large leeks

A splash of cooking oil

A few glasses of your favourite red wine

A sprinkle or two of salt and pepper

A splash of cream

SERVES FOUR

FEEL FREE TO TRY

You can use any liquid to braise the leeks, including white wine, orange juice, chicken broth or even water. The richness of the cream is optional. The leeks are just as wonderful without it.

HINTS

Keep the root end of the leeks intact. It makes them easier to handle when you rinse them. Dry them well before searing. They won't spatter as much and they'll brown more evenly.

BECAUSE VEGETABLES ARE LOADED with so many natural sugars, they easily develop the rich, full-bodied flavours of caramelization. Roast a few, throw in some briny feta and bright lemon, and even the kids will clean their plates!

128

ROAST VEGETABLES
WITH FETA CHEESE AND BASIL

2 zucchinis

1 eggplant

2 red bell peppers

1 or 2 onions

Half a cup or so of olive oil

A sprinkle or two of salt and pepper

The juice and zest of a lemon

A cup or so of crumbled feta cheese

A handful or two of basil leaves

SERVES SIX

Preheat your oven to 450°F (230°C). Cut the vegetables into large chunks, then toss with the olive oil, salt and pepper. Pour into a large baking pan and roast until caramelized and flavourful, about 1 hour. Stir the vegetables once or twice while they roast.

Remove from the oven and cool to room temperature.

Add the lemon to the cooled vegetables, then toss with the feta cheese and basil leaves. Serve immediately or refrigerate for up to a day or two.

FEEL FREE TO TRY

You can replace the lemon juice with a splash of balsamic vinegar.

HINTS

For best results the vegetables should snugly fill the pan. If they're spread too thinly, their juices will burn on the bottom. Too thick, and the bottom ones won't roast well.

BEETS ARE LOADED WITH earthy sweetness that matches well with the licorice-like flavours of fennel. Of course, they stain everything they touch, but that shows how good they are for you! Their deep colour indicates they are full of healthy antioxidants.

FENNEL-SCENTED BEETS

Preheat your oven to 350°F (180°C).

Quarter the beets and toss them with the oil, oranges, fennel seeds, salt and pepper. Pour them into a shallow baking dish and loosely cover the works with a piece of foil. Bake until the beets are tender—about an hour—then remove the foil and bake another few minutes until the liquid reduces to a syrup.

Serve immediately or refrigerate until cool. Before serving, toss with the parsley. Check out your red teeth!

5 or 6 washed, unpeeled beets

A generous splash of olive oil

The juice and zest of 2 oranges

A handful of fennel seeds

A sprinkle or two of salt and pepper

A handful of flat-leaf parsley leaves

SERVES FOUR TO SIX WITH LEFT-OVERS

FEEL FREE TO TRY

I prefer these beets cold, but they're also good straight out of the oven. For even more licorice flavour, try tossing in a handful of tarragon leaves with the parsley. Instead of fennel seeds, try another spice, such as cinnamon, cloves or cardamom.

HINTS

Peel the beets if you want, although it's not necessary; the skin has a coarse texture, but it's quite tasty. Put on a pair of kitchen gloves and cover your cutting board with a piece of plastic wrap to minimize cleanup. The foil helps keep the beets moist by trapping liquid while they bake. When the liquid reduces, its flavours concentrate.

I MAKE THIS DISH every fall, when locally grown squash and apples appear in the farmer's market together. It shows how well ingredients that grow together go together.

ACORN SQUASH WITH APPLESAUCE

2 acorn squash

A cup or so of Applesauce (page 159)

A few spoonfuls of soft butter

A sprinkle or two of salt and pepper

SERVES FOUR

Preheat your oven to 350°F (180°C). Cut the squash in half and scrape out the seeds. Place cut-side up in a baking dish. Add a large spoonful of applesauce to the centre of each one and top with a pat of butter. Season with salt and pepper.

Add a splash of water to the pan, then slide it into the middle of your oven. Bake until golden brown and caramelized, about an hour or so. Enjoy!

FEEL FREE TO TRY

Try sprinkling some of your favourite spice on the squash before baking. I like cinnamon, nutmeg, cardamom or star anise. For a tasty—but less decadent—version, replace the butter with olive oil.

HINTS

An oven temperature higher than 350°F (180°C) will burn the delicate squash before it cooks through. While the squash bakes it releases juices that pool on the bottom of the pan. They could burn and perfume the flesh with murky flavour, but adding water helps prevent that.

IF YOU LIKE GARLIC BREAD you'll love the rich mellow flavour of this version. Roasting the garlic first removes its intense pungency but retains its distinctive taste. It's just what you need to mop up tomato sauce from a pasta feed!

ROASTED GARLIC BREAD

133

Preheat your oven to 350°F (180°C). Slice the top off each head of garlic, exposing the cloves within. Wrap in foil. Use a serrated knife if you have one; it's easier. Place the garlic on a piece of foil and drizzle a bit of olive oil over each head. Enclose in the foil and bake until golden brown, about 30 minutes. Let the garlic rest for a few minutes, until it's cool enough to handle.

Grasp each head in the palm of your hand and squeeze the soft garlic into a bowl. You'll probably need to fish out a few stray pieces of peel. Add the butter, parsley and a touch of salt and pepper. Mix thoroughly.

Make a lengthwise cut into the bread loaf—along one side only—and open it up like a book. Spread half the butter onto the bottom half of the bread, then close the loaf and bake it until it heats through, about 10 to 15 minutes. Save the other half of the garlic butter for the next loaf. (Freeze it if you're not using it soon.)

4 heads of garlic

A few drizzles of olive oil

A stick of softened butter (4 ounces/125 g)

A handful of minced flat-leaf parsley

Salt and pepper

A loaf of Italian bread

SERVES SIX TO EIGHT WITH LEFTOVER BUTTER

FEEL FREE TO TRY

You can also slice the bread into thin rounds, spread each with butter and bake until toasted. Any leftover butter can be refrigerated and melted over your next steak dinner.

HINTS

I prefer flat-leaf parsley; it has a lot more herb-like flavour than its curly cousin. The foil helps keep the garlic from drying out as it bakes.

THESE ARE MY GOLD-STANDARD biscuits. My secret? Frozen butter! It's an old pastry chef's trick that has served me well. Butter tastes great and when it's frozen it becomes very easy to shred into the dough. After you try these a few times you'll be able to bake them in under 20 minutes— and clean up the mess too!

FROZEN BUTTER BISCUITS

134

4 cups (1 L) of all-purpose flour

2 tablespoons of baking powder

2 teaspoons of salt

2 sticks of frozen butter (8 ounces/250 g)

1 ½ cups (375 mL) of milk

A sprinkle or two of salt and pepper

MAKES EIGHT TO TEN LARGE BISCUITS

Preheat your oven to 400°F (200°C). Whisk the flour, baking powder and salt together until they're evenly mixed. Grate the frozen butter into the dry ingredients. Shred it through the large holes of a box grater or potato grater directly into the flour. Toss gently with your fingers until the butter shreds are spread evenly throughout the flour.

Pour the milk into the flour mixture and stir with the handle of a wooden spoon to form a dough mass. (The handle is gentler on the dough.) Fold the dough over a few times with your hands until all the ingredients come together. If necessary add a few spoonfuls more milk to help gather up any stray flour. This kneading will strengthen the dough a bit but not enough to toughen the biscuits. It will also help them form a crisp crust when they bake.

Pat the dough out on a lightly floured cutting board, forming a loose round shape. Cut into wedges—like a pie—or any other shape you're in the mood for. Position on a baking sheet, sprinkle on a bit of coarse salt and coarsely ground pepper. Bake for 15 minutes or so. You'll know they're done when they turn golden brown. Enjoy at once with lots of brown butter (page xx)!

FEEL FREE TO TRY

Biscuits are easily scented with herbs and spices. A spoonful or so adds lots of flavour. I tend to use aromatics that reflect the rest of the meal, but anything goes! Try dipping caraway biscuits into beef stew, or add a touch of nutmeg to your breakfast biscuits. Rosemary, thyme and even curry all taste great.

HINTS

Grated frozen butter doesn't bond with the flour; its tiny pieces stay separate and help make the biscuits light and fluffy. Too much kneading creates the stretchy gluten that makes bread strong—and biscuits tough. For maximum tenderness, avoid overworking the dough.

TREATS

AFTER ALL THAT HARD WORK cooking healthy food for your family, don't you deserve a treat? Of course you do! What do you feel like? An old favourite? Chocolate perhaps? No problem.

Treats are part of a good balanced lifestyle. It's okay to splurge a bit now and then! And when you do, you might as well have the best. Fruit, chocolate and rich dairy are all on my family's dessert menu. I love it when my son, Gabe, comes running for fresh-baked cookies! He doesn't have them every day so he sees them as treats.

Kitchen "science" really comes into play when you bake. But you can still experiment. Check out the hints and add your own insight for lots of flexibility. We're not talking about wedding cakes here!

Julia Child said it best: "Michael, everything in moderation—including moderation!" She loved treats!

BOTTOM ROW / LEFT TO RIGHT

I'M ADDICTED TO CHOCOLATE and always look for a way to work it into a treat, especially with coffee. Together they make mocha. Baked in coffee cups, this looks like a cup of coffee—until you cut into it! It always gets rave reviews.

A CUP OF HOT MOCHA

Preheat the oven to 325°F (160°C). Toss the chocolate and butter into a small bowl and set over a small pot of simmering water to begin melting it. The simmering water insulates the delicate chocolate from direct heat and keeps it from scorching. As it begins to melt, stir until smooth and remove from the heat.

Whisk the eggs, sugar, vanilla and coffee together. Add the chocolate mixture and whisk until smooth. Divide evenly between four coffee mugs.

Place the mugs in a small, high-sided pot. Add enough hot water around the cups to equal the level of the batter within the cups. Place in the oven and bake for 40 minutes. Serve immediately or cool and serve later.

4 ounces (125 g) of chopped bittersweet chocolate

1 stick of butter (4 ounces / 125 g)

4 eggs

Half a cupful of brown sugar

A spoonful of pure vanilla extract

Half a cupful of strong coffee, room temperature

MAKES FOUR MUGS

FEEL FREE TO TRY

You can leave out the coffee or bump up the chocolate flavour with a spoonful of cocoa powder. Try adding a few pinches of cinnamon, nutmeg or allspice.

HINTS

In a hot oven, an egg-filled batter can puff up and then collapse into a grainy mess. The water bath prevents that from happening by insulating the cakes from the direct heat of the oven. For the smoothest possible texture, let the batter cool to room temperature before baking it.

I DON'T HAVE A pastry chef on staff at my house, so I'm always on the lookout for an easy-to-make dessert like panna cotta. This Italian treat is smooth and light and can be flavoured with any herb, spice or liqueur. It's so simple to make that it will quickly become part of your repertoire.

140

PANNA COTTA

4 cups (1 L) of milk

A cupful of any sugar

2 spoonfuls of pure vanilla extract

A spoonful of your favourite spice or herb, or a splash of your favourite liqueur

2 packages of gelatin

MAKES SIX

Pour almost all the milk into a small saucepan and gently warm over medium heat. Stir in the sugar, vanilla and any optional flavours. Continue heating until the mixture just begins to simmer.

Meanwhile, sprinkle the gelatin powder over the remaining milk in a medium-sized bowl. Let it rest for a minute or two as it begins to rehydrate and absorb moisture. Pour in the hot milk and stir until completely dissolved.

Divide the mixture evenly between six small dessert moulds. Refrigerate until firm, at least 2 hours or overnight. To release the panna cotta from the moulds, gently loosen the edges, cover with a small plate, then flip over. Don't worry about leftovers!

FEEL FREE TO TRY

One of my favourite flavourings is a bit of minced rosemary. Its woodsy flavour is perfectly enhanced by the vanilla. Spiced rum, Grand Marnier, nutmeg and saffron are all tasty too. You can also substitute brown sugar, maple syrup or honey for the white sugar.

HINTS

Panna cotta simply means cooked milk in Italian. For moulds, look around the house; teacups and ramekins work best, but plastic cups can be trimmed to size. To help the panna cotta release easily, lightly oil the moulds before filling them.

LOOKING FOR A DESSERT you can prep in 10 minutes or less? Here it is! Not only are these baked apples easy to prepare, they're also easy to experiment with. I like to try out different spices every time I make them. Sometimes I even personalize each one with a different aroma! Try making 6 at a time.

142

SPICE BAKED APPLE

A baking apple, like Golden Delicious, Gala or Granny Smith

A sprinkle of a favourite spice, like cinnamon, nutmeg or allspice

A spoonful of brown sugar

A small pat of butter

SERVES ONE

Preheat the oven to 350°F (180°C) or if you're in a rush to 400°F (200°C). Roll the apple on its side and cut a small slice off the top. Save this hat. Scoop out the middle of the apple with a small spoon. Remove all the seeds and the woody core, but try not to punch through the bottom.

Sprinkle the middle of each apple with a light dusting of spice. Toss a spoonful of brown sugar into the centre; you don't need to fill it up completely. Add a dab of butter and replace the apple hat.

Place the apple in a baking pan and bake until heated through and soft, about 45 minutes or so. Serve with lots of vanilla ice cream!

FEEL FREE TO TRY

Use any spice that you enjoy. My family enjoys cinnamon, of course, but they also like star anise and cardamom. My son loves it when I place a cinnamon stick right in the centre of his baked apple.

HINTS

To minimize the clean-up, splash some water in the baking pan. It'll help keep the apple juices from burning in the oven.

JUST ABOUT ANY FRUIT can be cut, tossed with a bit of sugar, and baked with a crisp topping. There are as many ways to make that happen as there are cooks. Here's mine. It's perfect for experimenting and works year-round with whatever type of local fruit is in season.

FRUIT CRISP

Preheat your oven to 350°F (180°C). Toss the fruit with the brown sugar and the cornstarch. Load the works into a casserole dish.

For the topping, combine the brown sugar and oatmeal in a bowl. Grate the frozen butter into it and mix with your hands until it comes together into a crumbly mass. Crumble over the fruit, evenly covering it. Place the dish on a pan to catch any drips and bake until golden brown and bubbly, about 45 minutes to an hour.

FOR THE FRUIT

6 peaches, pears or large apples

OR

8 small apples

OR

12 plums or nectarines

OR

6 to 8 cups (1.5 to 2 L) of blueberries, strawberries or raspberries

A few spoonfuls of brown sugar

A few spoonfuls of cornstarch

FOR THE CRISP TOPPING

A cupful of brown sugar

A cupful of oatmeal

1 stick of frozen butter (4 ounces/125 g)

MAKES FOUR TO SIX SERVINGS WITH LEFTOVERS

FEEL FREE TO TRY

You can toss the fruit with your favourite spice. I like to use cinnamon, nutmeg or cardamom. You can also combine fruits and add other ingredients, such as nuts, raisins or other dried fruit.

HINTS

Instead of grating frozen butter into the topping, you can stir in melted butter; the texture of the topping will be a bit different, but it will still be crisp and tasty.

NOTHING WITH CHOCOLATE in it lasts long in my house, especially these quick-and-easy, nothing-fancy brownies. They're loaded with rich chocolate flavour and will easily satisfy the most discerning young palate. That is, if you can get them away from the grown-ups!

BROWNIES

12 ounces (375 g) of bitter-sweet dark chocolate

2 sticks of butter (8 ounces/250 g)

½ cup (125 mL) of flour

A pinch of salt

One spoonful of baking powder

4 eggs

A cupful of sugar

A big splash of pure vanilla extract

A cupful of chopped walnuts

MAKES 12 LARGE BROWNIES

Preheat the oven to 350°F (180°C). Toss the chocolate and butter into a small bowl set over a small pot of simmering water. This will insulate the delicate chocolate from direct heat and keep it from scorching. As it begins to melt, stir until smooth, then remove from the heat.

In a large bowl whisk the flour, salt and baking powder together until they're combined evenly. In a separate bowl, whisk the eggs, sugar and vanilla together, then stir in the chocolate. Stir in the dry ingredients and walnuts.

Lightly oil the bottom and sides of an 8 by 12-inch (2-L) baking pan. Sprinkle a bit of flour into the pan and shake until all the surfaces are evenly covered. Tap the pan upside-down on the counter to dislodge any extra. Pour in the batter and bake until set, about 40 minutes.

FEEL FREE TO TRY

For a richer chocolate flavour, try adding a spoonful of cocoa powder. Substitute your favourite nuts for the walnuts or leave them out altogether. For less chewy, more tender brownies, use pastry flour instead of all-purpose flour.

HINTS

The better the chocolate, the better the brownie. I prefer the richer flavour of bittersweet to the softer flavour of semi-sweet. Salt is important in desserts too. A pinch enhances the natural flavours of the chocolate.

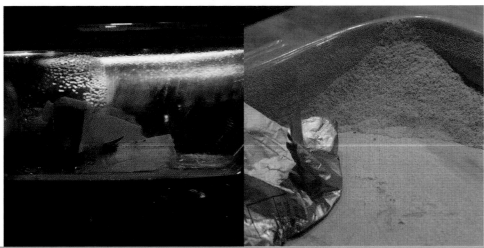

THIS IS PROBABLY the most important recipe in my repertoire because it impresses my son, Gabe, more than anything else I cook! It's a family favourite and I'm sure your family will love it too.

148

CHOCOLATE CHIP COOKIES

A heaping cupful of all-purpose flour

½ teaspoon of salt

1 teaspoon of baking powder

1 stick of cold salted butter (4 ounces/125 g)

⅓ cup (75 mL) of brown sugar

⅓ cup (75 mL) of white sugar

A spoonful of corn syrup

1 egg

A splash of pure vanilla extract

A cupful of chocolate chips

MAKES ABOUT 18 COOKIES (DEPENDING ON SIZE)

Preheat your oven to 375°F (190°C). Whisk the flour, salt and baking powder together. Set aside.

Cream the cold butter and sugars together, beating them until they're smooth in a countertop mixer. If you don't have a countertop mixer, beat vigorously by hand in a large mixing bowl, or combine them in a food processor. Add the corn syrup, egg and vanilla and continue beating until well combined. Scrape down the bowl and gradually add the flour mixture, beating just until combined. Stir in the chocolate chips with a spoon.

Using a spoon, scoop out a ball of the dough and drop it onto a lightly greased cookie tray. Flatten slightly. Repeat, leaving lots of room between the balls for the cookies to expand. Bake for 10 to 12 minutes. Cool for 2 minutes on the cookie sheet, then remove and cool on a rack.

FEEL FREE TO TRY

To save time you can whisk all the dry ingredients together, then melt the butter and whisk it in together with the other wet ingredients. The cookies will spread a bit more but will still taste wonderful. Try stirring in a cup of oats with the dry ingredients, or add walnuts or—my favourite–pine nuts with the chocolate chips. For a richer chocolate flavour, add a spoonful of cocoa powder to the dry ingredients. For an extra special treat substitute M&Ms for the chips!

HINTS

These cookies can be baked a few days in advance. Store them in a resealable plastic bag. The dough may also be frozen for several weeks and baked as needed. An insulated baking pan helps keep the bottoms from browning too fast. You can create your own by using two cookie sheets, one placed on top of the other.

HERE'S A CHEWY TROPICAL TREAT that's so easy to make you'll think you're forgetting something! I always make a big batch so there's a lot to share, but it's just as easy to cut the recipe in half. Your family and friends will love the addictive chewy texture and you'll love how quickly they can be made.

COCONUT MACAROONS

Preheat the oven to 350°F (180°C). Whisk the egg whites, vanilla, sugar and nutmeg together. Stir in the coconut and mix until it's well coated with the egg white mixture.

Moisten your hands. Form a large heaping spoonful of the mixture into a loose stack on a lightly oiled baking sheet. You can leave it craggy and irregular or pat it a bit to even it out. Repeat with the remaining mixture, leaving an inch or so between each pile.

Bake until golden brown, about 15 minutes. When they're done, they'll be firm to the touch but still a bit soft in the middle. When they first come from the oven they'll be a bit crumbly, but after 20 minutes or so of cooling they'll firm up nicely. Patience!

2 egg whites

A dribble of pure vanilla extract

Half a cupful of brown sugar

A small spoonful of nutmeg

1 ½ cups (375 mL) of unsweetened shredded coconut

MAKES TWELVE COOKIES

FEEL FREE TO TRY
Try sneaking other spices into the mix. Ground star anise, coriander and cardamom all add exotic flavour to the tropical coconut.

HINTS
Macaroons like to bake slowly. The oven is set high enough for the sugar to brown but not so hot it will burn. To prevent the cookie bottoms from browning too much, insulate the baking sheet by placing another sheet beneath it.

THIS STEAMING AROMATIC CIDER is a wonderful addition to any holiday party and is a perfect year-round warm-me-up. Its fragrant goodness will permeate your home with seasonal cheer. I guarantee your guests will ask for seconds–and the recipe!

WARM MULLED CIDER

Place the sugar in a tight pile in the centre of a large saucepot—large enough to hold the cider and wine. Pour the water around it and begin heating the works over high heat. Don't stir or shake the pot! The sugar mixture will quickly form a syrup and come to a boil. Continue simmering as the water boils away. When the syrup begins to brown around the edges, gently swirl it until the resulting caramel turns a beautiful golden brown. Working quickly—and carefully—add the cider to shock the caramel and prevent it from further browning. It will spatter, so be careful! Bring the entire mixture to a simmer.

Pierce the orange skin with the cloves, forming an even pattern, then add to the cider. Add the cinnamon, bay leaves, rosemary, star anise and vanilla. Continue simmering for another 30 minutes or so, until the cider reduces by a third.

Add the wine and bring the mixture back to a simmer. Serve immediately in a festive mug. Garnish each serving with a fresh rosemary sprig and a cinnamon stick.

A cupful of sugar

A cupful of water

8 cups (2 L) of fresh apple cider

An orange

A handful of cloves

A few cinnamon sticks

Several bay leaves

A branch or two of fresh rosemary

A handful of star anise pods

A splash of pure vanilla extract

A bottle of great Chardonnay or apple wine

FILLS A PUNCH BOWL AND SERVES SIX TO EIGHT

FEEL FREE TO TRY
Mulled cider is great with a shot of your favourite booze. Rum, whiskey and even liqueurs like Grand Marnier or Pernod work well, as does my favourite–a generous splash of port wine.

HINTS
When making caramel pouring water around the sugar helps the mixture cook evenly, forming a syrup, which evenly distributes the sugar and prevents it from burning.

MY BUDDY, PASTRY CHEF Thomas Haas, introduced me to this flavour combination. It seemed a bit odd at first—until I tasted it. The assertive flavour of cilantro perfectly matches the sweet tartness of a ripe pineapple. It's a match made in heaven—and in your kitchen!

154

PINEAPPLE WITH CILANTRO

A few handfuls of cilantro leaves

Half a cup or so of white sugar

A ripe pineapple, trimmed and cut into thin wedges

A generous sprinkle of shredded coconut

MAKES ENOUGH FOR FOUR TO SIX DESSERTS

Reserve a few cilantro leaves and toss the rest, along with any stems, into the bowl of a food processor. Add the sugar and pulse until they become a gritty, sandy, almost-puréed mixture.

Toss the pineapple with most of the sugar mixture, reserving some to sprinkle on top of each portion. Serve in bowls, topped with the remaining cilantro leaves and a sprinkle of grated coconut.

FEEL FREE TO TRY

You can substitute fresh basil for the cilantro—its strong aromas and sweet flavour also complement pineapple.

HINTS

For a touch more flavour, toast the sugared pineapple in a 350°F (180°C) oven for a few minutes until it lightly browns.

THIS STEAMING MUG of hot cocoa is my favourite winter treat. A touch of cayenne pepper complements the temperature of the brew but doesn't make it too spicy. It's a surprising twist that adds just the right exotic edge.

HOT HOT COCOA

Pour everything into a small pot and whisk until well combined. Bring to a simmer over medium heat. Whisk a little more to froth it up a bit.

Pour into your favourite mug and find a comfy chair to enjoy it in!

FEEL FREE TO TRY

To add a hint of aromatic spice that perfectly complements the cocoa, stir in a few pinches of cinnamon, nutmeg, cloves, allspice or cardamom. Using honey instead of sugar adds a floral aroma that goes well with the cocoa. Add ground coffee and strain after a few minutes for a java treat.

HINTS

Cocoa is loaded with antioxidants, which makes it—and real chocolate— good for you! Dark chocolate has more cocoa and more flavour than most other types.

A cup or so of milk

A heaping spoonful of cocoa powder

A heaping spoonful of brown sugar

A handful of dark chocolate chips

A dribble of pure vanilla extract

A tiny pinch of cayenne pepper

SERVES ONE

JARS

A LOT OF THE THINGS I cook make more sense in bigger batches than small ones. Condiments and sauces. Flavours to enjoy alone or in other dishes. They fill the clear glass jars that clutter my kitchen and are always ready to help out a meal!

Jars are easy to fill. I refrigerate them so I don't have to bother with the mad-scientist sterilizing thing. No worries. They'd be good for a month or more–if they lasted that long! Jars get better with time. Their edges soften while their flavours mature. They age gracefully.

Jars are easy to share. I often fill a few for friends. The best way to get invited back for barbecue is to leave a little reminder behind!

These jars are fun to play with. Try adding your own flavours and make them yours!

THIS BRIGHTLY FLAVOURED CONDIMENT traditionally highlights the delicate flavours of fish with the energetic punch of sharp horseradish and bright lemon. Try it. You'll want to make it yourself every time!

COCKTAIL SAUCE

A 28-ounce (796-mL) can of whole ripe tomatoes

Several large heaping spoonfuls of horseradish

A small can of tomato paste

The juice and zest of 2 lemons

A spoonful or two of Worcestershire sauce

As much red pepper sauce as you like

A sprinkle or two of salt

MAKES ONE JAR

Blend everything in the food processor or blender. Don't make it too smooth though—leave it slightly chunky.

Dip away!

FEEL FREE TO TRY
For a touch of complementary herb flavour, add a handful of minced fresh dill, cilantro or basil.

HINTS
Unless it's tomato season in my backyard, I prefer the field-ripe flavour of canned tomatoes to the bland hardness of their fresh cousins.

BUTTER ALWAYS TASTES GOOD, but for a real treat, try browning it first. You'll be amazed at how this simple transformation adds flavour! This spread is great with toast, pancakes or anywhere else you enjoy a bit of butter.

BROWN BUTTER SPREAD

4 sticks of room temperature butter (1 lb/500 g)

MAKES ABOUT 2 ½ CUPS (625 ML)

Toss 1 stick of butter into a small saucepot and heat it until it melts. Because butter contains as much as 20 percent water it will begin to steam and foam. Once the water has evaporated the foam will subside and the temperature will begin to rise past the boiling point of water. The milk fat solids that make up 1 or 2 percent of the butter will then begin to brown.

Continue heating as the butter begins foaming a second time. Swirl it gently, watching the colour, until it turns golden brown and releases the aroma of toasting nuts. Immediately pour the browned butter into a bowl to stop it from browning further. Cool to room temperature. Be patient—this will take at least an hour.

Whip the remaining butter in a countertop mixer, then drizzle in the cooled brown butter. Whip until fluffy.

FEEL FREE TO TRY
For a complementary aromatic spice, add a pinch or two of nutmeg to the butter as you whip it.

HINTS
If the browned butter doesn't fully cool to room temperature, it will melt the other butter and the mixture won't whip well.

IN THE FALL, WHEN APPLES are in peak season, I always make a giant batch or two of applesauce and freeze it. It's so easy that my son, Gabe, helps out! All winter long it reminds my family of our favourite season. Any apple makes great applesauce but my favourites are McIntosh and Golden Delicious.

APPLESAUCE

Remove the cores from the apples, leaving the skin on. Cut them into several large chunks. Toss into a pot and add the sugar, cinnamon, vanilla and salt. Add a splash of water, just enough to cover the bottom of the pot, and place over medium-high heat. Cover with a tight-fitting lid.

Stir frequently. In a few minutes the water will begin to steam and the heat will encourage the apples to soften and release their own moisture. When the apples have all softened and the mixture simmers, it's done, about 20 minutes in total.

For a rustic, chunky consistency pass the sauce through a food mill or force it through a colander with the back of a spoon. For a smoother version, purée in a food processor or blender, then pass through a strainer. In either case the skins will be left behind and should be discarded.

A dozen of your favourite apples

A cupful of brown sugar

A heaping spoonful of cinnamon

A dash of pure vanilla extract

A pinch of salt

MAKES 4 CUPS

FEEL FREE TO TRY

Many spices complement apples. Try nutmeg, allspice, cloves or cardamom. Some herbs are very tasty too. I enjoy rosemary, thyme and even bay leaf.

HINTS

There are many types of apples; each behaves differently when cooked. Some will soften and break down quickly, while others will take longer. Keep an eye on the pot and stir frequently so they don't stick to the bottom.

THIS CLASSIC SAUCE, with its deep caramel flavour, turns anything into instant dessert. Every time I transform bland white sugar into rich, slightly bitter caramel I get excited. I think it's magical how much flavour a simple cooking process can add! Your family will too.

BUTTERSCOTCH SAUCE

160

A cupful of white sugar

A cupful of water

1 stick of butter (4 ounces/ 125 g) cut into a few pieces

A cupful of cream

A dribble of pure vanilla extract

MAKES 2 CUPS OR SO

Pour the sugar into a small, tight pile in the middle of a saucepot. Add the water, pouring it around the pile, then begin heating over high heat. Don't stir! The water and sugar will quickly combine and form a simple syrup. As the heat increases it'll begin simmering and steaming and the water will gradually evaporate. Once it's gone the steam will die down and the temperature will begin to rise, leaving behind a pure melted-sugar syrup.

As the heat continues to rise, the sugar will start to turn pale golden. When you see the first hint of colour, gently swirl the pan to keep the colour even. When it's a deep golden brown add the butter and whisk it in until the sauce is smooth. This will drop the temperature out of the sugar browning range.

Add the cream and vanilla and whisk until smooth. Pour into a jar and refrigerate until thickened.

FEEL FREE TO TRY
For a touch of grown-up flavour you can add a splash of your favourite rum or liqueur to the sauce before cooling it.

HINTS
Don't stir the sugar syrup. If you do, small bits of sugar will splash on the side of the pot, then dry and fall back into the syrup where they'll crystallize and turn the whole syrup gritty.

IF YOU LIKE FLAVOUR as much as I do you'll love this traditionally made ketchup. It's packed with so much aromatic goodness that you'll forget about buying supermarket ketchup. It's the best way to jazz up a burger and fries!

KETCHUP

Toss all the ingredients into a large saucepan. Place over medium heat and bring to a simmer. Continue cooking, stirring occasionally, until the mixture reduces by half, about 30 minutes.

If you have an immersion blender, purée the mixture in the pot until it's smooth. If you don't, use a regular blender, but cool the ketchup to room temperature before puréeing it. (An agitated hot liquid always expands violently; it'll explode all over your kitchen and make a huge mess!)

Get some french fries and start dipping!

A 28-ounce (796-mL) can of chopped tomatoes

A small can of tomato paste

A large chopped onion

A cup of red wine vinegar

Half a cupful of sugar

Half a cupful of olive oil

2 heaping spoonfuls of nutmeg

2 pinches of ground allspice

2 or 3 bay leaves

A sprinkle or two of salt and pepper

MAKES ABOUT 2 CUPFULS

FEEL FREE TO TRY
If you're a fan of garlic, toss a whole head of peeled cloves into the pot. After it's reduced, try adding your favourite hot sauce until the ketchup is pleasingly spicy.

HINTS
Stand a wooden spoon in the pot and mark the ketchup's level on it. Use that mark as a reference to know when the mixture has reduced by half.

THESE EASY-TO-MAKE tomatoes are a tasty addition to any salad, pasta or vegetable dish. They also make a great snack. The drying process dramatically intensifies the flavour of bland, store-bought winter tomatoes. My son calls them tomato candy!

OVEN-DRIED TOMATOES

A dozen or so plum tomatoes

Olive oil for drizzling

A sprinkle or two of salt and pepper

MAKES 24 DRIED TOMATOES

Preheat your oven to 400°F (200°C). Slice the tomatoes in half lengthwise, then toss them with a generous splash of olive oil, salt and pepper. Loosely arrange them skin side down on a lightly oiled baking sheet.

Place in the oven, then turn the heat down to the lowest possible setting and begin drying. After a few hours have a peek. Because ovens—and tomatoes— vary, it may take 6 to 8 hours in total, or even overnight. You'll know they're done when they shrink noticeably, lose their fleshiness and taste amazing.

FEEL FREE TO TRY

Plum tomatoes have less moisture than other varieties so they're perfect candidates for drying. Of course, any tomato deserves to have its flavours concentrated, so use whatever variety you have on hand.

HINTS

It doesn't take very much heat to brighten the taste of a tomato. A low setting–250°F (120°C)–is perfect to dehydrate them and concentrate their flavours.

A GOOD HOME-MADE chicken broth can be a lifesaver. It's easily turned into a soup, sauce, stew or side dish, and its unmistakable hearty richness just can't be duplicated with what's in the carton or can at the grocery store. I keep some on hand all the time.

CHICKEN BROTH

163

Roughly chop the vegetables into small chunks, then toss them into a saucepot or stockpot with the chicken and bay leaf. Cover with a few inches of water, then bring the works to a boil over high heat. Reduce the heat to low and continue simmering for 2 hours or so.

Pass through a strainer and voila—chicken broth! Lightly season with a pinch or two of salt and pepper.

A large onion

A large carrot

A few stalks of celery

A large package of fresh chicken wings

A bay leaf or two

A sprinkle or two of salt and pepper

MAKES 1 LARGE JAR

FEEL FREE TO TRY
For a heartier broth, roast the chicken wings in a 400°F (200°C) oven until they're golden brown and richly flavoured. Be sure to dissolve every bit of the browned juices on the bottom of the roasting pan—add a shallow layer of water and let it rest for 20 minutes or so before scraping it and adding it to the simmering broth. You can also use the leftover carcass from a roast chicken dinner instead of the wings.

HINTS
Chicken wings are very high in the natural gelatins that add lots of body to the broth. By cutting the veggies relatively small you encourage them to easily release their flavours into the simmering broth.

THIS IS THE CLASSIC PESTO GENOVESE featuring basil, pine nuts and Parmesan. It's a perfect accompaniment for white meats, fish or pasta. Because the word "pesto" simply means paste, you can use many different ingredients to make this tasty condiment.

BASIL PESTO

A few large handfuls of fresh basil

Half a cupful of grated Parmesan or Romano cheese

A few handfuls of pine nuts

A generous splash or two of extra virgin olive oil

A sprinkle or two of salt and pepper

MAKES ABOUT A CUP

Toss everything into a food processor and purée until smooth.

FEEL FREE TO TRY
Toss in a few garlic cloves for pungent strength. Try experimenting with different herb, cheese and nut combinations such as mint, goat's cheese and pistachio; or sage, goat's cheese and walnut.

HINTS
The olive oil helps get everything spinning in the food processor. Because it also adds flavour, this is a good place to use your very best oil.

THIS ALL-PURPOSE CONDIMENT is a great way to add a splash of Thai flavour to a salad or vegetable dish. The secret to its exotic flavour is its perfect balance of sweet, sour, salty and spicy tastes.

SPICY THAI PEANUT SAUCE

Half a cupful of smooth peanut butter

The juice and zest of 4 limes

A small spoonful of chili flakes or hot sauce

A couple of big spoonfuls of honey

A couple of big spoonfuls of soy sauce

A couple of big spoonfuls of water

A large bunch of mint

A handful of peanuts

MAKES ABOUT 2 CUPS

Toss everything into your food processor or blender. Purée until almost smooth, leaving the peanuts a touch chunky. This sauce will stay fresh in your refrigerator for several weeks.

FEEL FREE TO TRY
If you like the strong flavour of fresh cilantro, use it to replace some or all of the mint. For even more authentic Thai flavour add a splash of Thai fish sauce.

HINTS
Some blenders are stronger than others; if yours needs a little help, add a splash of water to help it purée the thick peanut butter.

THESE TASTY ONIONS lose all their pungency in the pickling process but gain a sweet sharpness that makes them a great last-minute addition to any salad. They're a great multi-purpose condiment and are delicious with any type of fish.

PICKLED RED ONIONS

Slice the onions as thinly as possible. To make this easier, cut them in half and lay them on their cut side before slicing them further. Cram the sliced onions into a large Mason jar.

Pour the sugar and vinegar into a small pot and bring to a boil with the salt and pepper. Pour the hot syrup over the onions; cover them and refrigerate overnight before use.

2 large red onions

A cupful of sugar

A cupful of red wine vinegar

A sprinkle or two of salt and pepper

MAKES ABOUT 2 CUPS

FEEL FREE TO TRY

You can aromatize the pickling liquid with a spoonful of your favourite herb or spice. Try bay leaves, fennel seed or even ground juniper berries.

HINTS

Because sugar and vinegar are such great preservatives, these pickled onions will last indefinitely in your refrigerator. They're at their best after a day or two, once their flavours have had a chance to mature.

THANKS!

HI EVERYBODY! Thanks for everything you did to help make this book so special. I can't fit everyone's name in but our collective spirit flavours every page!

Thank you Rachel and Gabe for inspiring me to be my best—in life and in the kitchen.

Thank you Gretha and Johanna, my partners, for our shared vision, Trevor for your quiet creativity, and Edward for your leadership. Thank you Karen, Anna and Food Network Canada for playing ball with us. Thanks Jill for keeping us all in line.

Thank you Art and Dean for lugging all that production gear everywhere and Dugald for showing 'em where to put it! Thanks Jim, Patti, Tommy and Dave for making it all look so easy. And thanks to everybody else on the team for putting up with us.

Thank you Ann and Ann, Sherrill, Carla and Tracy; Erin, Allie and Alex; Alanna and Loretta; Pat and Cory and anyone who ever washed a dirty dish for me.

Thanks to Atlantic Wholesalers and the Superstore for sponsoring our show and this book. It's my favourite place to find all the great food my family loves!

And thank you—our audience—for supporting our genuine efforts. I'm humbled to share my show, this book and my life with you.

SPECIAL CREDITS

Alanna Jankov, *Alanna's Photography*–Principal Photographer
Loretta Campbell, *Eastern Eyes*–Assistant Photographer
Rachel Leslie–Food Styling
Tommy Archibald–Food Styling
David Jenkins–Food Production

INDEX

INDEX

INDEX

INDEX